Selected Translations

Also by W.S. Merwin

The Mays of Ventadorn, 2002
The Lost Upland: Stories of Southwest France, 1992
Unframed Originals: Recollections, 1982
Houses and Travellers, 1977
The Miner's Pale Children, 1970

TRANSLATIONS

Sir Gawain & the Green Knight, 2002
Purgatorio, 2000
East Window: The Asian Translations, 1998
Pieces of Shadow: Selected Poems of Jaime Sabines, 1996, 2007
Sun at Midnight (Poems by Musō Soseki) (with Sōiku Shigematsu), 1989, 2013
Vertical Poetry (Poems by Roberto Juarroz), 1998
From the Spanish Morning, 1985
Four French Plays, 1985
Selected Translations, 1968–1978, 1979
Euripedes' Iphigeneia at Aulis (with George E. Dimock Jr.), 1978
Osip Mandelstam: Selected Poems (with Clarence Brown), 1974
Asian Figures, 1973
Transparence of the World (Poems by Jean Follain), 1969, 2003
Voices (Poems by Antonia Porchia), 1969, 1988, 2003
Products of the Perfected Civilization (Selected Writings of Chamfort), 1969
Twenty Love Poems and a Song of Despair (Poems by Pablo Neruda), 1969
Selected Translations, 1948–1968, 1968
The Song of Roland, 1963
Lazarillo de Tormes, 1962
Spanish Ballads, 1961, 2008
The Satires of Persius, 1961
Poem of the Cid, 1960

ANTHOLOGY

Lament for the Makers: A Memorial Anthology, 1996, 2010

W.S. MERWIN

Selected Translations

1948–2011

COPPER CANYON PRESS

Port Townsend, Washington

Cover art: *Structure of Thought 17*, © Doug and Mike Starn, 2012; ARS NY

Copper Canyon Press is in residence at Fort Worden State Park
in Port Townsend, Washington, under the auspices of Centrum.
Centrum is a gathering place for artists and creative thinkers
from around the world, students of all ages and backgrounds, and
audiences seeking extraordinary cultural enrichment.

LIBRARY OF CONGRESS CATALOGING-IN-PUBLICATION DATA

Selected translations 1948–2011 / [compiled by] W.S. Merwin.

p. cm.

ISBN 978-1-55659-409-0 (alk. paper)

1. Poetry—Collections. 2. Poetry—Translations into English.

I. Merwin, W.S. (William Stanley), 1927–

PN6101.L25 2012

808.81—dc23

2012025545

3 5 7 9 8 6 4 2

FIRST PRINTING

COPPER CANYON PRESS

Post Office Box 271

Port Townsend, Washington 98368

www.coppercanyonpress.org

CONTENTS

Selected Translations
1948–1968

This volume is in memory of
Laurence G. Sampson
who first taught me to love another language

~

CONTENTS 1948–1968

6

As the title indicates, these translations are taken from the work of twenty years. The originals are native to widely scattered periods and poetic conventions. I can speak only subjectively of what the extremes share.

They were not all undertaken with the same ostensible purpose. Some are testimony to old affections that have survived such representation. Many are relics of the same kind of search that prompts us, in our time, to read translations of poems: a wish to embrace, even through wrappings, poetry that was written from perspectives revealingly different from our own. Some of them were commissioned.

I began translating with the idea that it could teach me something about writing poetry. The great exemplar, of course, was Pound. The neo-Flaubertian image of poetry as a "craft" was in all the ikons I could see. Unfortunately something of the "how" of writing poetry is probably always important, a reminder of the ambivalences of our imperfection and our artifice. And every way of learning it, and the learning itself as it is acquired, has peculiar dangers. Translation may be no more dangerous than any other to a growing recognition of the true original that, in del Vasto's words, "tastes of the source." It is love, I imagine, more than learning, that may eventually make it possible to be aware of the living resonance before it has words, to keep the distinction clear between mere habit and the style that is some part, at least, of the man, and will impel one to be wary of any skill coming to shadow and doctor the source, any deftness usurping the authority it was reared to serve. "When I pronounce men to be quick of hearing," Chuang Tzu wrote, "I do not mean that they hearken to anything else, but that they hearken to themselves." Which of course, is the true and exacting vocation of the poet's ear, a matter of origin before it is one of learning. But every time the words are found, the finding is a contribution to learning as well, and it may be in the interest of clarity if some of the learning is obviously distinct from the particular source in oneself.

When I was still at college I made the pilgrimage to St. Elizabeth's to see Pound. He spoke of the value of translation as a means of continually sharpening a writer's awareness of the possibilities of his own language. He meant English, not any personal idiom of mine (I knew perfectly well that I had none at the time), and I still approach translation as a relatively anonymous activity in which whatever in the result may appear to be mine comes there simply because that is how the language, in the always elaborate given circumstances, sounds most alive to me. Pound also urged—at that point and to me, at least—the greatest possible fidelity to the original, including its sounds.

And I have not come to use translation as a way of touching off writing that then became deliberately, specially, or ostentatiously my own. On the contrary, I have felt impelled to keep translation and my own writing more and more sharply separate. This has been true not only when I knew enough of a language to be able to approach the original, up to a point, on my own, but also in those translations from languages which I do not know at all, in which I have had to rely on intermediary parsings and impressions, with the extra risks that that involves.

I must make clear what part of this collection falls into that second category. The only languages outside English in which I have any proficiency at all are Romance languages, particularly French and Spanish. But I long ago forgot most of what Latin I ever learned, and more recently most of what Portuguese I ever knew; my reading Italian (which was all I had) was never anything but laborious and uncertain. So the Persius, for example, was composed with the help of every previous translation I could find, and whatever line-by-line notes I could lay hands on, and was then gone over by a scholar; I could certainly not have managed it with nothing but the text and a dictionary. And as for the other languages—I know no Chinese, and the translations are from other versions. Where I could I used several other versions, and where possible I preferred to work from a previous translation in some language other than English, which would be less likely to afford suggestions. I managed to do this with most of the poems from languages I don't know at all. The Welsh and Irish poems, for instance, in their present forms, are based on French rather than on English forebears. No one who wants to read those poems for the purposes of scholarship is likely to be interested in my versions anyway, but I have not wilfully gone farther from what I thought was the original sense than the translations from which I was working had done. The same is true of the Greek poems, though there I occasionally condensed in the interests of a sharpness that I did not think was a disservice to the original. The poems from the more exotic and from the "primitive" languages were all taken from French or Spanish translations, except the Vietnamese poems, which were done in collaboration with Nguyen Ngoc Bich, who supplied the literal English. I have forgotten almost all of the little German I once knew, and the versions of German poems were made with the help of bilingual editions and a dictionary, except for the Bobrowski poem, which was translated in collaboration with Jean-Pierre Hammer. The Tyutchev, Blok, Esenin and Mandelstam poems were translated in collaboration with Olga Carlisle, and the Brodsky poems in collaboration with Wladimir Weidlé.

W.S.M.

Death is before me today
like health to the sick
like leaving the bedroom after sickness.

Death is before me today
like the odor of myrrh
like sitting under a cloth on a day of wind.

Death is before me today
like the odor of lotus
like sitting down on the shore of drunkenness.

Death is before me today
like the end of the rain
like a man's homecoming after the wars abroad.

Death is before me today
like the sky when it clears
like a man's wish to see home after numberless years of captivity.

1960

Liu Ch'e | Chinese
140–87 B.C.

Oh the sound of her silk sleeves
no longer
oh the dust deepening
in the jade courtyard
the vacant room cold
abandoned
the doors
double-barred and their bars
littered with fallen leaves
oh if anyone looks now
for the beauty
of that woman where can it be found
I feel my heart
to which rest will not come

1967

Li Po | Chinese
701-762

QUIET NIGHT THOUGHTS

I wake and my bed is gleaming with moonlight

Frozen into the dazzling whiteness I look up
To the moon herself
And lie thinking of home

1966

Niu Hsi Chi | Chinese
8th century

Where the mist has torn
The hills are the colors of spring
The sky is whitening
Not many stars are left
The fragment of moon is going out
But your face in the early light
Glitters
Now we must separate

After all the words
Nothing is eased
Turn your head I have something to add
You will remember
My skirt of green silk woven loosely
The new grass will remind you of it everywhere

1966

Tu Fu | Chinese 8th century

AUTUMN NIGHT

The dew falls, the sky is a long way up, the brimming waters are quiet.
On the empty mountain in the companionless night doubtless the
    wandering spirits are stirring.
Alone in the distance the ship's lantern lights up one motionless sail.
The new moon is moored to the sky, the sound of the beetles comes to
    an end.
The chrysanthemums have flowered, men are lulling their sorrows
    to sleep.
Step by step along the veranda, propped on my stick, I keep my eyes on
    the Great Bear.
In the distance the celestial river leads to the town.

1962

THE LAKE OF THE TEN THOUSAND MOUNTAINS

I throw the line in from this little island.
The water is clear and my heart is protected.
The fish pass under the trees of the lake.
Along the promontory monkeys swing on the vines.
The wandering beauty of former days took off her necklace
in these mountains, the legend says.
I look for her but I have not found her.
The songs of the rowers lose the way to the moon.

1962

Khong Lo

Vietnamese
medieval, Ly dynasty
died 1119

THE IDEAL RETREAT

I will choose a place where the snakes feel safe.
All day I will love that remote country.
At times I will climb the peak of its lonely mountain
to stay and whistle until the sky grows cold.

1967, translated with
Nguyen Ngoc Bich

Ngo Chi Lan | Vietnamese 15th century

AUTUMN

Sky full of autumn
earth like crystal
news arrives from a long way off following one wild goose.
The fragrance gone from the ten-foot lotus
by the Heavenly Well.
Beech leaves
fall through the night onto the cold river,
fireflies drift by the bamboo fence.
Summer clothes are too thin.
Suddenly the distant flute stops
and I stand a long time waiting.
Where is Paradise
so that I can mount the phoenix and fly there?

1968, translated with
Nguyen Ngoc Bich

WINTER

Lighted brazier
small silver pot
cup of Lofu wine to break the cold of the morning.
The snow
makes it feel colder inside the flimsy screens.
Wind lays morsels of frost on the icy pond.
Inside the curtains
inside her thoughts
a beautiful woman.
The cracks of doors and windows

all pasted over.
One shadowy wish to restore the spring world:
a plum blossom already open on the hill.

1968, translated with
Nguyen Ngoc Bich

Anonymous | Vietnamese
18th century

A WOODCUTTER ON HIS WAY HOME

Here and there little breezes stir the rushes.
At dusk the birds hurry as though they were lost.
Loaded with wood he moves slowly homeward.
He moves slowly, knowing the way.

1967, translated with
Nguyen Ngoc Bich

Anonymous | Vietnamese folk poem

THE SUBSTITUTED POEM OF LAUREATE QUYNH

This is what the professor wrote home, listen:
Tell my wife not to get heated up.
I have got it all the way north here perfectly limp.
Down south there she had better look to her clam.
Is it still tight and winding like a gopher's burrow
or is it gaping by now like a catfish grotto?
Tell her to hang on to it even if it gives her a fight.
I will be home in a couple of days.

1967, translated with
Nguyen Ngoc Bich

Anonymous | Kabylia folk poems

I want someone to go out to the plain
work till evening
come back with the others
look in at the window to see what she is doing
fall between her thighs
and she will wake even if she is not sleeping.

~

God of this year, I implore you,
you that are angry with me
as though I had killed your father,
you gave flour to everybody
except me. To me you left
bran, saying, Take that or nothing.
I beg you by Saint Moulani, pity me
O my God,
angry as though I had smashed up a holy place.

~

O sun rising
who light everything
in the name of God please
show me how to get to you
so I can arrive some day
now the suffering has stopped
or else it will start again.

1967

Anonymous | Kabylia
folk song

BERBER SONG

She has fallen in the dance,
None of you knows her name.
A silver amulet
Moves between her breasts.

She has hurled herself into the dance.
Rings chime on her ankles.
Silver bracelets.

For her I sold
An apple orchard.

She has fallen in the dance.
Her hair has come loose.

For her I sold
My field of olive trees.

She has hurled herself into the dance.
Her collar of pearls glittered.

For her I sold
My orchard of fig trees.

She has hurled herself into the dance.
A smile flowered on her.

For her I sold
All my orange trees.

1962

Anonymous | Dahomey

FIVE SONGS OF DAHOMEY

The time will come even yet when we will dance there
And we will say look there are the girls we will marry
And the sky will clear.

~

We were dispersed one by one and the dry season came.
And we will come back again and we will meet.
The man who has no field, when he dances nobody knows it.

~

Night is turning into day
And the clouds are being swept across the sky.
Those who will buy you are twisting the ropes for you.

~

Early in the morning I say goodbye to those who have cut down
     the big tree and I put on my gear and I say that I am
     setting out on a journey.

Death is in this country from his hole to his head and you put
     on your gear and you say that you are setting out on
     a journey?

~

Tomorrow I will be lying on the terrace
And they find me dead and the sun goes down
And goes in, red, shining,
And the hyena is restless but he will turn back.

1961

TATAR SONGS

I

The sun rises going the rounds
as though it were tied to the apple tree.
One day if we live we will be back
making the rounds like the sun.

II

Little finger painted with henna, little copper fingernail, dice
    of gold,
is it possible to leave a lover in this world?

Because of the orchard the sun does not pass my window.
As for me I have turned yellow, shrivelled by love.

Do not whiten the roof tree of the low house.
I am alone, I am unhappy, do not be cruel to me.

Why do you look out the door all the time?
I would give my life for the darkness of your eyes.

The child of the *bai* drinks water from a golden cup.
Under the moon a cloud, the moon's child.
And I, I have turned yellow, withered by love.

III

My beloved, the face is covered with blood.
The falcon's face, covered with blood.
The wind blew, a curl of hair came loose.
A wick took it, and the face covered with blood.

I built a house and it was a mirage.
But it was a shelter for my whole life.
The point of my stick was not solid
and our night had its danger.

I am dying because I always watched the road.
I looked to right and to left.
Neither you nor I will ever be done
watching the road, watching the road.

The seas turn into horses
and cupbearers.
I drank to quiet my sorrow
but it grew wilder all the time.

1962

Anonymous | Roumanian
folk poem

SONG FOR THE DEAD

The evening becomes evening.
No one will shelter you.
And at that time
The otter will come toward you
To make you afraid.
But do not be afraid.
Receive her as your sister.
The otter knows
The order of the rivers,
The lay of the fords,
Will get you across,
Will save you from drowning,
Will carry you
To the cold sources
To refresh you
After the shudder of death.

Also before you
The wolf will appear
To make you afraid.
But do not be afraid.
Receive him as your brother.
The wolf knows
The order of the forests,
The grain of the paths,
He will lead you
On the level road
To a king's son,
To paradise

Where life is good,
The hill for playing:
There is your place;
The field of peonies:
There is your heart.

1960

Anonymous | Eskimo

Into my head rose
the nothings
my life day after day
but I am leaving the shore
in my skin boat
It came to me that I was in danger
and now the small troubles
look big
and the ache
that comes from the things
I have to do every day
big

But only one thing
is great
only one
This
In the hut by the path
to see the day
coming out of its mother
and the light filling the world

1967

The dead who climb up to the sky
climb up steps
to the sky
up worn steps
all the dead who climb up to the sky
on worn steps
worn from the other side
worn from the inside
climb up to the sky

1967

Anonymous | Quechua
             | Peru

ICHI THE DWARF

In Qjelle Huanca the earth opened and a dwarf popped out. He was naked and his hair was bright red like a fire. He sat down on a stone, and for the fun of it he brandished his lighted hair. His little lively eyes, like small coals, stared at the landscape in wonder, and because it was cold he began to cry like a sucking pig.

Then that little dwarf began to leap around among the rocks and crags and his scarlet hair caught in the thick leaves and fig branches and tangled him. At midnight he beat his belly like a drum and the raw sound rebounded from hill to hill. In the quiet afternoons he blew on his pipe and the flute warbled and trilled, but what he liked best of all was to frighten the men working in the fields. Whenever he found them gathering wood he would growl, he would give a low growl.

He sang, too, under the ground, and his songs went up into the air in the same way that the water of the marshes turns into clouds. When dawn rose into the heavens the faraway songs of the little dwarf Ichi woke the children, and the calves lowed sweetly.

1959

THE RAINBOW

There was a fine rain at daybreak. The whole sky began to shine. The rainbow was born out of a marsh and he bent like a great bow from Pocyaccho to Pitacchopis.

He is afraid of the stares of men, which are too quick and piercing for him, and he retreats into the sky like a string of colors.

Some boys went to look for his feet. His toes are made of crystal, so he can hide them, and the boys could not find them. Then the boys threw stones at the rainbow.

When he enters the body of a man or a woman they become very sick
and to cure them they are given a ball of seven-colored wool to unwind.

1959

ARAWI

I have lost my dove.
Wandering, I call to her in a loud voice.
Everyone who finds me says,
"Why did you love her?"
Where have you flown?
Whom have you left here to console me?
Like a dove whose wings have been cut off
I will die walking back and forth.
Come back, dove whom I cherished.
How long must I wait for you?
In the nest, where we should be,
Now the birds of night raise their moans.

1959

BEAN FLOWER

Bean flower,
Black and white,
Like the heart of that man
Who loves two women.

Long live the apple.
Its tears are sweet.
This world has reason
To be bitter.

Little star of heaven
Lend me your brightness,

For the life of this world
Is a dark night.

1959

MY SPOUSE CHUNAYCHUNAY

My spouse, Chunaychunay,
Sweetly you carry me.

And what you say to me is sweet.
You, Wichiri,
Your cruel father
Stole from my mother
Her horses and saddled mules.

You wander by the river
With a blazing club
Abusing me because I am an orphan.
In the midst of many
Rags I sleep.
I live among miseries.

For your sake I will go.
Thus I sleep, I sleep.
Your net catches two abreast,
Rain, giver of water.

O Chunaychunay, brotherly heart,
Portion of the great feast
Which now will never return.
Do nothing to me, Putti,
For today my heart was brought to tears.

1959

Anonymous | Caxinua
Amazon

THE CREATION OF THE MOON

The man cut his throat and left his head there.
The others went to get it.
When they got there they put the head in a sack.
Farther on the head fell out onto the ground.
They put the head back in the sack.
Farther on the head fell out again.
Around the first sack they put a second one that was thicker.
But the head fell out just the same.
It should be explained that they were taking the head to show to
        the others.
They did not put the head back in the sack.
They left it in the middle of the road.
They went away.

They crossed the river.
But the head followed them.
They climbed up a tree full of fruit
to see whether it would go past.

The head stopped at the foot of the tree
and asked them for some fruit.
So the men shook the tree.
The head went to get the fruit.
Then it asked for some more.

So the men shook the tree
so that the fruit fell into the water.
The head said it couldn't get the fruit from there.
So the men threw the fruit a long way

to make the head go a long way to get it so they could go.
While the head was getting the fruit
the men got down from the tree and went on.

The head came back and looked at the tree
and didn't see anybody
so went on rolling down the road.

The men had stopped to wait
to see whether the head would follow them.
They saw the head come rolling.

They ran.
They got to their hut they told the others that the head
was rolling after them and to shut the door.

All the huts were closed tight.
When it got there the head commanded them to open the doors.
The owners would not open them because they were afraid.

So the head started to think what it would turn into.
If it turned into water they would drink it.
If it turned into earth they would walk on it.
If it turned into a house they would live in it.
If it turned into a steer they would kill it and eat it.
If it turned into a cow they would milk it.
If it turned into wheat they would eat it.
If it turned into a bean they would cook it.
If it turned into the sun
when men were cold it would heat them.
If it turned into rain the grass would grow and the animals would crop it.

So it thought, and it said, "I will turn into the moon."
It called, "Open the doors, I want to get my things."
They would not open them.
The head cried. It called out, "At least give me

my two balls of twine."
They threw out the two balls of twine through a hole.
It took them and threw them into the sky.

It asked them to throw it a little stick too
to roll the thread around so it could climb up.

Then it said, "I can climb, I am going to the sky."
It started to climb.

The men opened the doors right away.
The head went on climbing.
The men shouted, "You going to the sky, head?"
It didn't answer.

As soon as it got to the sun
it turned into the moon.
Toward evening the moon was white, it was beautiful.
And the men were surprised
to see that the head had turned into the moon.

1962

THREE PAMPAS INDIAN SONGS

If I have two horses
we will go one on each

If I have only one
I will take you behind me

I am very poor
but we will go

We will travel ten days.
The length of this country!

I don't say it will be tomorrow
that we will go

But we will go.

~

When I was a good and quick little girl
they treated me like a treasure

oh heart!

Many suns and many moons I saw
time passes

oh heart!

How I have changed. I am not a girl now
I am very old

oh heart!

What is the use of grieving
if nobody will listen

oh heart!

~

Necessity has made us all very poor.
The best families could not keep their riches.
If a poor man comes to a hut he sees the hearth cold.
And he hears, "I am poor. I do not even have fire any more."

We bury the dark thought in the ashes
And say nothing, not to add to our trouble.
They have taken everything from us: land, family,
Flocks, soul. Now we do not even have fire.

1958

Myrddyn | Welsh
ca. 6th century

YSCOLAN

Your horse is black your cloak is black
your face is black you are black
you are all black—is it you Yscolan?

I am Yscolan the seer
my thoughts fly they are covered with clouds.
Is there no reparation then for offending the Master?

I burned a church I killed the cows that belonged to a school
I threw the Book into the waves
my penance is heavy.

Creator of living things you
greatest of all my protectors forgive me.
He that betrayed you deceived me.

I was fastened for a whole year
at Bangor under the piles of the dam.
Try to think what I suffered from the sea worms.

If I had known what I know now
the liberty of the wind in the moving treetops
that crime could not be laid to me.

1962

Anonymous | Welsh
ca. 6th century

THE GLORY OF TALIESIN

Messengers came to me they crowded up to me
to tell my heart of the war tomorrow.

The drink of Beli is like the foam the oar lifts at sea.

Like a bright shield is the back of a shadow
like anger and indignation
out of a city where nine hundred governors are dead.

There will be a battle at Menao fierce vengeance
and on Conwy cliff a fight without mercy

cold death will be the lot of the Muse
it is natural to love her.

To the violence of the blows of Edern's sword
three men will fall who could not be dissuaded

three fleets on the great current
will foretell the day of darkness
and three nights of battle across
three noble countries.

The ships will be coffins

three from each of the three
three sins
and the mountain of Eryry will be the hill of darkness.

Three will be one army of Saxons a second a third.

In the country of Kymrys widowhood
is waiting for the wives.

At Kynon's arrival look for the fire to break out.
Kadwaladyr will mourn for him
he will visit his own torment on the countryside
burning the straw and the roofs.

After that a marvelous thing.
From a man and his brother's daughter
steel will be born
the line of Anarawd.
From him will descend the Red
the wise the cunning
who will neither spare nor defend
brother nor cousin.

At the sound of the warrior's horn
nine hundred will lose hope
as disaster arrives everywhere.

You will see your glory grow leaves
however your heart may have been oppressed.

1962

Anonymous | Welsh
ca. 7th century

DEATH SONG OF KYNDYLAN

White village in the woods
its grass covered with blood
all the time ever since it was built.

White village ever since it was built
blood lay on the green around it
under the feet of its warriors.

White village in the valley
would have celebrated a battle won.
Have the people who lived there come home?

White village between Tren and Throdwyth
saw shields broken
instead of oxen resting.

White village between Tren and Travel
saw blood on its grass
instead of its fallow under the plow.

1962

Anonymous | Irish
12th century

THE SONG OF CELLACH

I greet the white morning
stepping on the earth like a flame,
I greet its sender,
the new morning, the conqueror.

White morning in your pride,
brother of the bright sun,
I greet you, white morning,
lighting my book.

My marked book tells me
my life hangs in the balance,
I am afraid of Malcroin,
he that will strike me.

Hooded crow, hooded crow,
gray cloak, sharp beak,
I know what you want,
you're no friend of Cellach.

Croaking raven,
bird, if you're hungry,
wait in the castle;
you'll dine on my body.

The kite from the cliff of Cluain Eo
will come hungry to the brawl,
he'll hook me in blue talons,
he'll hang on.

The fox in the dark wood
will be with them, he wastes no time,
he'll eat my blood and flesh
in cold crevices with one entrance.

The wolf in the castle
that's east of Druin meic Dair
in one hour will be standing over me,
head of the pack.

I had a dream,
it was Wednesday night:
the wild dogs dragged me
east, west, through the red ferns.

I had a dream
they took me into a valley,
four of them held me,
I think they did not bring me back.

I had a dream
my followers took me to their house
and poured out a drink for me
and drank to my health.

Oh little wren with hardly a tail,
shame, shame: did you sell your song?
Coming to warn that I'm here,
and ending my life.

1962

SONG OF EXILE

Already the month
of May and the spring,
almost summer;
branches swell, flowers
open; now he who is not
in his own place
longs to go to his country,
saddles his horse at night,
spends the dark hours
over the horseshoes, makes
silver shoes for his horse,
nailed with gold nails, puts on
spurs, sword on his belt; the girl
who loves him
is holding a candle
so he can see, in one hand
the candle, in the other
the wineglass; each time
she fills it again for him
she says again, "Master,
take me, take me with you, take me
where you go, I
will cook so you can eat,
make the bed so you can sleep,
be earth so you can walk on me,
a bridge so you can cross over,
a goblet of silver
for you to drink wine from,
for you to drink your

wine from, and see
my reflection in."
"Where I am going, little one,
is beyond women.
Wolves hold the mountains
and thieves the passes
to lay hands on you, girl,
and make me a slave."

1960

MAIDO

Maido is there, Maido
in a palace of mirrors
holding a mirror
up to her beauty,
oh beauty
standing like a cypress;
all of one evening she wanted
Costas in bed with her.
"Here I am, Maido, I've come.
I'm not afraid of John.
John's off on the mountain,
he's gone hunting stags,
I hope to God it rains and snows
and the Danube overflows
and carries all the bridges away
and John on the mountain.
I hope to God the bears eat him."
And they are still there talking
and here is John, come home
with a load of stags, with a train
of live stags and tame bears,
with the reins of his horse hauling trees
torn up by the roots.
He spurs his horse to the door.
"Maido, come down, get the meat."
"John, I'm afraid of the stags,
and I'm more afraid of the bears.
Take them to your mother.
They don't frighten her."

So he rides to his mother's. "Mother,
come down, Mother, open the door,
and get the meat. Maido
is afraid of the stags,
and she's more afraid of the bears."
"She's not afraid of the stags,
it's not the bears she's afraid of.
She's afraid because she's deceived you,
and Costas is there with her."
With one foot he smashes the door
and she falls limp in a corner.
"Costas, you devil's baby,
what's your excuse?"
"It's your Maido; she called to me
from the window."
He takes out his little knife
and cuts off her head.
On a silver plate he carries it
to his mother-in-law.
"Mother-in-law, come down
and see what I've brought you."
She laughs as she goes to uncover it,
then she covers it, weeping.
"Oh, what have you done,
dog, murderer, head
for curses to ride on!
And what are courtrooms for?
You could have taken her there.
And what are judges for?
They could have judged her."
He puts the head in a little bag,
takes it to the miller.
"Good mill, grind, grind
Maido's head to coal dust,
to coal dust to make
black bread,

to coal dust
to make ink
so that those who can write
can write the head of Maido."

1960

Anonymous | Greek
four poems

LIBERTY

Down there
on the shore
down there
on a beach
there is an eagle lying
weighted with snow
and he calls on the sun
to shine: Shine my old sun
shine
my golden eye
so the snow will
melt and my wings
be free
and I will fly
like the other birds
and write a message
and send it to the desert
to my palaces
my high
dwellings

EXILE

In a foreign country
wear black
the heart does

THE CRYPTS

Here
in this church
put away
the girls sleep
lemon trees
the boys sleep
cypresses
the old men sleep
torn up by the roots
the women sleep
splintered doors
the children sleep
dried apples

SWALLOW

A swallow
from the white sea
starts saying: March March
February
old friend old fright
snow snow
rain rain
never mind
you too smell the spring

1967

Catullus | Latin
ca. 84-ca. 54 B.C.

Salutations, girl with nose none of the smallest
Nor exquisite foot nor eyes quite like jet
Nor delicate fingers nor mouth any too clean
Nor a tongue notable for its elegance,
Mistress of that dissipated Formian.
You pass for a beauty in the provinces?
They compare you with my Lesbia?
Oh foolish and unlicked generation!

1958

Let us live, my Lesbia, and let us love;
As for the buzzings of censorious
Old men, let them be all one for us.
Suns can endure their settings and return
But for us once our short light is gone
Night is a sleep from which we never wake.
Give me a thousand kisses, then a hundred,
Another thousand and another
Hundred, and another, and more thousands
Till we have lost all count, so that those
Who'd fix us with their evil eyes
Can't turn the count of our kisses against us.

1958

Like a god he seems to me who beholds you,
Even greater than the gods, if that could be,
Who sits facing you, and everlastingly
        Gazes, and hears

Your sweet laughter which in my wretchedness
Uproots all my senses; Lesbia, you no more
Than appear before me, and at once I have
        No voice in my mouth,

My tongue is benumbed too, and a thin flame
Slips through my limbs, my ears begin ringing
With a din of their own, and twofold night
        Falls on my eyes.

Catullus, idleness is your undoing.
From idleness you grow overwrought, you flare up
Too much. Kings have been lost, and rich cities,
        Through idleness.

1958

Caelius, my Lesbia, Lesbia, that same
Same Lesbia, whom alone Catullus,
More than himself and all that he owned, loved,
Now at street corners and in alleys milks
The scions of high-minded Remus.

1958

Furius and Aurelius, bound to Catullus
Though he penetrate to the ends of the Indies
Where the eastern ocean crashing in echoes
      Pours up the shore,

Or into Hyrcania, soft Arabia,
Among Tartars or the archers of Parthia,
Or where the Nile current, seven times the same,
      Colors the waters,

Or through the beetling Alps, by steep passes, should come
To look on the monuments of great Caesar,
Gaul, the Rhine, and at the world's bitter end
      The gruesome Britons,

Friends, both prepared to share with me all these
Or what else the will of heaven may send,
To my mistress take these few sentiments,
      Put none to nicely:

Let her spread for her lechers and get her pleasure,
Lying wide to three hundred in one heat,
Loving none truly but leaving them every one
      Wrung out and dropping;

But as for my love, let her not count on it
As once she could: by her own fault it died
As a flower at the edge of a field, which the plow
      Roots out in passing.

        1958

Persius | Latin A.D. 34-62

THE SIXTH SATIRE

Has the season, descending into winter,
Fetched you, by now, Bassus, to your Sabine fireside?
Is your strung harp alive to the chastening plectrum,
Oh artisan without peer at ordering in verse
The primal elements of our language and waking
The virile tones of the Latin lyre, oh marvelous
Old man, alive with the merriment of youth and with
Songs, besides, which are gay without being dirty.
For the moment the Ligurian coast and my own
Winter sea offer me their little warmth; from a breach
In the bastion of towering cliffs at the sea's edge
A deep valley here runs inland. As Ennius put it:
"Citizens, you would do well to know the harbor
Of Luna"—speaking in his right mind, when he had
Done dreaming that he was Homer, the Lydian,
Descendant of Pythagoras's peacock.
           Here I live, neither troubled by the multitude
Nor flustered by the south wind's ill humors menacing
My flocks, nor miserable because that corner
Of my neighbor's fields is richer than my own. Even
Though men whose birth was beneath mine were to grow rich,
Every one of them, I would still not get all hunched up
And scrawny with fussing over it, nor go without
Sauce for my meat, nor descend to sniffing the seals
Of wine jars to see whether the rank stuff could possibly
Still be swallowed. People aren't all alike. You get twins, with
The same horoscope, turning out to have different
Temperaments. One man has a habit (but only
On birthdays) of sprinkling his dry greens with brine
Which the sly fellow buys by the cupful—and you can tell

By the way he dribbles the pepper onto the platter
That the stuff is holy. Here's another, a large-mannered
Young man who will shortly have eaten his way through
A huge inheritance. As for me, I try
To make the most of things, without being so lavish
As to feed my freedmen on turbot, nor of so
Sophisticated a palate that I can tell
Hen thrush from cock thrush by the taste.
        Live on your own harvest, mill your own grain, that's as it
Should be. Why should you worry? You have only
To harrow again to have another crop on the way.
But obligations nag at your elbow: there's that
Friend who washed up on the Bruttian rocks, in the wreckage
Of his ship, and hauled himself in. He's penniless.
His possessions, accompanied by his useless prayers,
Have settled under the Ionian Sea, and he himself
Is stretched on the beach with the great statues of the gods
From off the vessel's stern strewn round him, while already
The gulls are gathering on the splintered ship's timbers.
Why not divest yourself of a plot of good farmland
And give it to the unfortunate man, and save him
From toting his picture around on a blue board?
Are you hesitant because your heir would be angry
At a cut like that in the property, and after holding
A cheap funeral supper over you, would stuff your bones
Unperfumed into the urn, never bothering
To make sure that the cinnamon was fresh and the cassia
Unmixed with cherry, merely mumbling, "Thought you could
Shave bits off your estate and get away with it,
Did you?" And Bestius will drone on, libelling
The sages of Greece: "That's how it goes, ever since
That neutered brand of philosophy was imported
Into this city with the dates and pepper, our
Farmhands have been getting dainty. Now they've taken
To polluting their gruel with rich oil." But why
Should you worry about this sort of thing once you're on

The other side of the fire? As for you, my heir,
Whoever you are, leave the crowd for a minute and lend me
Your attention.
                              Haven't you heard, friend? A laurelled
Dispatch has arrived from Caesar, announcing
Victory, the pick of the Germans routed—and already
They're sweeping the dead ashes from the altars, and
Caligula's wife is seeing to the arrangements:
Bouquets of arms for over the gates, costumes for kings,
Yellow wigs for prisoners, and chariots, and monstrous
Models of the Rhine. I'm putting on a little show
Myself, to celebrate the occasion and the gods
And the Emperor's guiding spirit—with a hundred pairs
Of gladiators. Well who says I shouldn't? Who
Would dare to say I shouldn't? God help you if you don't
String along! Oh, and I'm having a largesse of bread,
And meat, and oil distributed to the populace.
Any objections? Speak up. "Oh no," you say, "not with that
Field full of stones within easy range." Because even
If none of my father's sisters are left, and
I survive all my cousins, and my father's brother
Leaves no great-granddaughters, and my mother's sister
Dies without issue, and my grandmother is survived
By no other descendant, I can always take myself
Over to Bovillae, to the hill of Virbius
Where there's a wonderful selection of beggars, and there
I'll find me an heir in no time. Manius, for example—
"A son of the soil?" Well ask me who my own grandfather's
Grandfather was. Maybe I can tell you, though again
It might take a moment. But carry it back one more
Generation, then another, and sooner or later
You'll end up with a son of the soil. So if you're going to be
Clannish and stuffy about it, this Manius is really
A sort of great-uncle indefinitely removed.
Besides, you've got a nerve, when you're ahead of me, grabbing
For my torch before I've finished my race. Think of me

As your private Mercury, for I come to you like
That god (in the pictures) with a money bag in my hand.
Don't you want it? Are you determined not to be happy
With what I leave you? "It's not all here." All right, I spent
Some of it for my own uses, but whatever's left
Is all yours. Only you'll get nowhere if you expect me
To give an account of every cent I inherited
Ages ago, from Tadius. And don't come plying me
with fatherly maxims about investing capital
And living on the interest. "But what will be left?"
Left? Here, boy, don't lose a minute: pour out the oil.
Pour, I said! I want my cabbage drowned in it. Maybe
You think I'm going to confine myself on holidays
To smoked cheek of pork and split pig's ear garnished with nettles
So that on some future occasion a prodigal unripe
Sot, my heir, his guts stuffed with goose livers, and the fretful
Vein in his privates setting up a restive throbbing,
May piss into a high-born pussy. Or that I should
Abstain till I'm diaphanous so that his paunch
Can jiggle like a priest's.
                              Go, peddle your soul
For lucre, and haggle, and drag the ends of the earth for
Merchandise. See to it that no one outdoes you
At slapping the fat of Cappadocian slaves, up on the
Auction block. Turn every penny into two. "I have. And
Into three. And four. I've got it up to ten." Well, make
A mark where you want me to stop and I'll inform Chrysippus
That you're the man to finish his unfinishable pile.

1959

Clothe him, in garments
They clothe him, with great sorrow,
For today he departs
From his house and where he was born.

Clothe him, in garments
They clothe him, with many laments,
For the blow struck in rage
Found no cure nor balm.

Clothe him, in garments
They clothe him, with many sighs,
The young men depart,
There is none who will bring up his sons.

Clothe him, in garments
They clothe him, with much grief,
The young men depart
And leave his house empty.

1957

Do not throw earth
On his lovely face,
For today he departs
From his house and his people.

Do not throw earth
On his colored eyes;
The young men go away,
None will bring up his darlings.

1957

Anonymous Spanish
Middle Ages

LAMENT

On a dark night
My mother bore me.
They wrapped me in mourning.
Good luck I had none.

When I was born
The hour was waning,
No dog was heard,
No cock crowing.
No cock crowing,
No dog was heard,
Only my fortune
Cursing me.

Go, leave me,
You that are lucky;
Lay eyes on me
And ill luck will dog you.
When I was born
Omens foretold:
"If he loves women
He will eat scorn."

A sign of night
I was sired under:
Saturn reigning
In waning orbit.
My milk and cradle
Are the hard ground,
A bitch bore me,
No woman, no woman.

My mother, dying,
With sorrowing voice
By name named me
A luckless son.
Love, in a fury,
With his liegemen,
His bow in his hands,
Stands in my way.

Too great my love
Of your beauty,
Too great my sorrow;
Good luck I had none.

1957

Anonymous | Spanish

MEDIEVAL LYRICS

>   In Avila, my eyes
> In the town of Avila.

>   In Avila by the river
> They killed my lover,
> In the town of Avila.

~

> I see they all lament.
> I shall die silent.

~

> My mother
> Sent me to draw water,
> Alone, and at such an hour.

~

> The beekeeper kissed me.
> By the taste of honey I knew it was he.

~

> Do not go out at night to go hunting, sir.
> Because the night is dark, fair love.
> And I die of fear.

~

> Fine rain falling
> And the night dark
> And the shepherd a green boy.
> I will not be safe.

~

She has lovely eyes
Which she never raises.

~

At the wedding
Everyone is singing
And the bride weeping.

1958

Anonymous | Spanish
late Middle Ages

FOURTH *ROMANCE* OF THE SEVEN PRINCES OF LARA

In sorrow I abide in Burgos,
Blind with weeping at my misfortunes,
Not knowing when the day rises
Nor when the night has come,
Were it not that with hard heart
Doña Lambra, who hates me,
Each day as the dawn breaks
Sends to wake my grief also:
So that I may weep for my sons
One by one, every day
She has her men throw
Seven stones at my window.

1957

MELISENDA

If you know the pains of love,
In your grace, in your goodness,
Knight, if to France you go,
Ask for Gaiferos,
And tell him that his lady
Commends herself to him,
That his jousts and tourneys
Are famous among us,
And his courtliness
At praising the ladies.
Tell him for a certainty
That they will wed me:

Tomorrow I must marry
One from across the sea.

1958

THE ENCHANTED PRINCESS

    The knight has gone hunting, hunting,
As often before,
His hounds are weary,
He has lost his falcon.
Against an oak he leaned,
It was marvelously high;
On a branch at the top
He saw a little princess;
The hair of her head
Covered all of that oak tree.
"Knight, do not be afraid,
Nor draw back with dread,
For I am the good King's daughter,
My mother is Queen of Castile.
Seven fairies bewitched me
In my nurse's arms
To remain for seven years
Alone on this mountain.
It is seven years today,
Or at dawn tomorrow.
Knight, in God's name I beg you,
Take me away with you,
To be your wife if you please,
Or if not, your mistress."
"Wait for me, my lady,
Until dawn tomorrow.
I will go to my mother nearby
And ask her to advise me."

The girl gave him an answer,
These are the words she spoke:
"Oh knight, you are wrong and foolish
To leave me here alone!"
But he goes to get advice
And leaves her on the mountain.
The advice that his mother gave him
Was to take her for his mistress.
When the knight returned to the place
He could not find the princess.
He saw a great procession
Bearing her away.
The knight, when he beheld it,
Fell down onto the ground,
And when he came to his senses
The words he spoke were these:
"The knight who could lose such a thing
Deserves a heavy penance.
I will be my own judge,
I will pronounce my own sentence:
Let them cut off my feet and hands
And through the town drag me."

1957

Anonymous | Spanish versions at different periods

THE PRISONER

It was May, the month of May,
When warm days are with us,
When the grain gets its growth
And the fields are in flower,
When the skylark sings
And the nightingale gives answers,
When those who are in love
Go in love's service,
Except for me, wretch, living
In sorrow in this prison,
Not knowing when it is day
Nor when night has come
Except for a little bird
Which sang to me at dawn;
A man killed it with a crossbow,
God give him an ill reward!

1957

DON GARCÍA

     Don García is walking
Along the top of a wall,
With arrows of gold in one hand
And a bow in the other.
He calls down curses on Fortune,
He recounts her abuses:
"When I was a child the King reared me,
God was a cloak around me;
A horse and arms he gave me
Excelling all others;
He gave me Doña María
To be my wife and consort,
He gave me a hundred maidens
To wait upon her,
He gave me the Castle of Uraña
As her dowry,
He gave me a hundred knights
To keep the castle,
He provided me with wine,
He provided me with bread,
He provided me with sweet water,
For there was none in the place.
The Moors laid siege to me there
On Saint John's Day in the morning.
Seven years have come and gone
And the siege has not been lifted.
I have seen my people die
Because I had nothing to give them.
I set them up on the ramparts

With their weapons in their hands
So that the Moors should think
That they were ready for battle.
In the Castle of Uraña
There is only one loaf of bread.
If I give it to my children
What then of my wife?
If I were so base as to eat it
They would not forgive me."
He broke the bread into four pieces
And flung it down into the camp.
One of the four pieces
Rolled to the King's feet:
"Allah, here is grief for my Moors!
Allah is pleased to afflict them.
From his castle's overabundance
He supplies our encampment."
And he bade them sound the trumpets
And they lifted their siege.

1958

THE GRAY SHE-WOLF

As I was in my hut
Painting my shepherd's crook
The Pleiades were climbing
And the moon waning;
Sheep are poor prophets
Not to keep to the fold.
I saw seven wolves
Come up through a dark gully.
They cast lots as they came
To see who should enter the fold;
It fell to an old she-wolf,
Gray, grizzled, and bowlegged,
With fangs lifting her lips
Like the points of knives.
Three times she circled the fold
And could take nothing;
Once more she went round it
And snatched the white lamb,
The Merino's daughter,
Niece of the earless ewe,
Which my masters were saving
For Easter Sunday.
"Come here, my seven pups,
Here, my bitch from Trujilla,
Here, you on the chain,
Run down the gray she-wolf.
If you fetch back the lamb
On milk and bread you will dine;
Fail to fetch her back,
You'll dine on my stick."

On the heels of the she-wolf
They wore their nails down to crumbs;
Seven leagues they ran her
On the harsh mountains.
Climbing a little ravine,
The she-wolf begins to tire:
"Here, dogs, you can take the lamb,
As sound and well as ever."
"We do not want the lamb
From your wolving mouth;
Your skin is what we want,
For a coat for the shepherd,
Your tail to make laces
To fasten his breeches,
Your head for a bag
To keep spoons in,
And your guts for lute strings
To make the ladies dance."

1957

Anonymous | Catalan
post-Renaissance

THE CORPSE-KEEPER

Seven years I have kept him, dead
And hidden in my chamber.
I change the shirt on him
Every holiday of the year.
I have anointed his face
With roses and white wine.
I have watched his bones laid bare
Of their white white flesh.
Alas, what can I do,
Wretch, in my disgrace?
Should I tell my father
He would say it is my lover;
Should I tell my mother
I would have no peace after;
Should I tell my sister
She knows nothing of love;
Should I tell my brother
He is the man to kill me;
Should I tell the constable
He would have me punished.
Better for me to say nothing,
To endure it and hold my tongue.
One day at my balcony,
Looking from my window,
I saw a huntsman passing
Who hunts in our crags.
"Huntsman, good huntsman,
One word, hear me:
Will you bury a dead body?

You will be rewarded.
And not in worthless coppers
But in gold and silver."
Going down the stairs
Two thousand kisses I gave him:
"Farewell, delight of my life,
Farewell, delight of my soul;
It will not be long
Before I come and visit you."

1957

LAMENT FOR THE DEATH OF GUILLÉN PERAZA

Grieve, ladies, so may God keep you.
Guillén Peraza remained in Palma,
Withered, the flower of his face.

No palm are you, you are broom,
You are cypress of mournful bough,
You are misfortune, dire misfortune.

May molten stone buckle your fields,
May you see no pleasures, only sorrows,
May the sandpits cover your flowers.

Guillén Peraza, Guillén Peraza,
Where is your shield, where is your spear?
By ill fortune all is ended.

1958

Lope de Vega | Spanish 1562-1635

In Santiago the green
Jealousy seized me,
Night sits in the day,
I dream of vengeance.

Poplars of the thicket,
Where is my love?
If she were with another
Then I would die.

Clear Manzanares,
Oh little river,
Empty of water,
Run full of fire.

1950

Go, sighs,
Go there where you go always,
And if she is sleeping, my little one,
Forget her.

1950

SPANISH FOLK SONGS

Throw a crust to the dog
if you come to see me
because my mother sleeps as lightly
as a hare.

~

When they broke the news to me
that you've stopped loving me
even the house cat
looked at me and laughed.

~

You tell them everywhere
that I love you
and I loathe even the saint
you were named for.

~

I can't go to church
because I'm a cripple.
I'm going to the tavern
little by little.

~

We say goodbye to each other.
We say it again, sadly.
My heart hangs from the bars
of your balcony.

~

I am getting tired
of your love
because there aren't many chances
and you waste them.

~

If you don't come
to your window tonight
number me among the dead
in the morning.

~

I forsook father and mother
to go with you
and you left me alone
on the road.

~

Fancy hairdo
full of kiss-curls
and not even four chairs
in the house.

~

Little pearl, suit yourself when you marry:
your parents will die
and won't come from the other world
to see if you're happy.

~

God bless me, Father Adam,
how I love that woman!
The day I don't see her
I draw her picture on the wall.

~

Little beauty,
since I saw that calm face
the wings of my heart have fallen
over my feet.

~

Heart, I told you before,
and twice, and three times,
don't knock at that door.
No one will answer.

1957

Juan Ramón Jimenez

Spanish
1881–1958

I shall run through the shadow,
sleeping, sleeping, to see
whether I can come where you are
who died, and I did not know.

Wait, wait; do not run;
wait for me in the dead water
by the lily that the moon
makes out of light; with the water
that flows from the infinite
into your white hand!
               Wait;
I have one foot already through the black
mouth of the first nothing,
of the resplendent and blessed dream,
the bud of death flowering!

1949

León Felipe | Spanish
1884–1968

I AM GOING BECAUSE THE EAR OF WHEAT
AND THE DAWN ARE NOT MINE

I have walked, lost, over the world, asking for bread and light.
And the sun is bread and light!
Look how he rises from the oven and ascends into the dawn for all,
with his double crown of flour and crystal!…
O ancient and generous God, banished by man!
You, always there, unfailing in the ear of wheat and in the dawn
and I here hungry and blind, with my beggar's cry lost again and again
   throughout history!

1960

THE DEAD

The first thing I forgot was your voice.
Now if you were to
speak here at my side
I would ask, "Who is that?"

After that I forgot your footstep.
If a shadow were to gutter
in the wind of flesh
I would not be sure it was you.

One by one all your leaves fell
before a winter: the smile,
the glance, the color of your clothes, the size
of your shoes.

Even then your leaves went on falling:
your flesh fell from you, your body.
I was left with your name, seven letters of you.
And you living,
desperately dying
in them, body and soul.
Your skeleton, its shape,
your voice, your laugh, seven letters, those letters.
And repeating them was your only life, your body.
I forgot your name.
The seven letters move about, unconnected,
unknown to each other.
They form advertisements in streetcars; letters
burn at night in colors,

they travel in envelopes shaping
other names.
There, everywhere, you go too,
all in pieces by now, dismantled, impossible.
There goes your name everywhere, which was you,
risen
toward various stupid heavens
in an abstract alphabetical glory.

1966

Federico García Lorca | Spanish 1898–1936

THE LITTLE MUTE BOY

The little boy was looking for his voice.
(The king of the crickets had it.)
In a drop of water
the little boy was looking for his voice.

I do not want it for speaking with;
I will make a ring of it
so that he can wear my silence
on his little finger.

In a drop of water
the little boy was looking for his voice.
(The captive voice, far away,
put on a cricket's clothes.)

1954

HE DIED AT SUNRISE

Night of four moons
and only one tree,
only one shadow
and only one bird.

I track through my flesh
the trail of your lips.
The fountain kisses the wind
without touching it.

I bear the No that you gave me
in the palm of my hand,

like a wax lemon
almost white.

Night of four moons
and only one tree.
My love is spinning
on the point of a needle.

1954

CASIDA OF THE DARK DOVES

Through the branches of the laurel
I saw two dark doves.
The one was the sun,
the other the moon.
Little neighbors, I said to them,
where is my tomb?
In my tail, said the sun.
In my throat, said the moon.
And I who was walking
with the earth at my belt
saw two eagles of marble
and a naked girl.
The one was the other
and the girl was no one.
Little eagles, I said to them,
where is my tomb?
In my tail, said the sun.
In my throat, said the moon.
Through the branches of the laurel
I saw two naked doves.
The one was the other
and both were no one.

1954

GACELA OF THE LOVE THAT HIDES

Only to hear
The bell of La Vela
I crowned you with a crown of verbena.

Granada was a moon
Drowned among grasses.

Only to hear
The bell of La Vela
I tore up my garden in Cartagena.

Granada was a doe,
Pink, through the weathervanes.

Only to hear
The bell of La Vela
I burned in your body
Not knowing whose it was.

1954

Jorge Luis Borges | Spanish 1899–1986

PARTING

Three hundred nights like three hundred walls
must rise between my love and me
and the sea will be a black art between us.

Time with a hard hand will tear out
the streets tangled in my breast.
Nothing will be left but memories.
(O afternoons earned with suffering,
nights hoping for the sight of you,
dejected vacant lots, poor sky
shamed in the bottom of the puddles
like a fallen angel…
And your life that graces my desire
and that run-down and lighthearted neighborhood
shining today in the glow of my love…)

Final as a statue
your absence will sadden other fields.

1968

THE GENEROUS ENEMY

> *In the year 1102, Magnus Barfod (the name means "barefoot") undertook the general conquest of the Irish kingdoms; it is said that on the eve of his death he received this greeting from Muirchertach, the King of Dublin:*

May gold and the storm fight on your side, Magnus Barfod.
May your fighting meet with good fortune, tomorrow, on the fields of
my kingdom.

May your royal hands strike awe, weaving the sword's web.
May those who oppose your sword be food for the red swan.
May your many gods sate you with glory, may they sate you with blood.
May you be victorious in the dawn, King who tread upon Ireland.
May tomorrow shine the brightest of all your many days.
Because it will be your last. That I swear to you, King Magnus.
Because before its light is blotted out I will defeat you and blot you out,
    Magnus Barfod.

1968

Pablo Neruda | Spanish 1904-1973

WALKING AROUND

As it happens, I am tired of being a man.
As it happens I go into tailors' shops and movies
all shrivelled up, impenetrable, like a felt swan
navigating on a water of origin and ash.

The smell of barber shops makes me sob out loud.
I want nothing but the repose either of stones or of wool,
I want to see no more establishments, no more gardens,
nor merchandise, nor eyeglasses, nor elevators.

As it happens I am tired of my feet and my nails
and my hair and my shadow.
As it happens I am tired of being a man.

Just the same it would be delicious
to scare a notary with a cut lily
or knock a nun stone dead with one blow of an ear.
It would be beautiful
to go through the streets with a green knife
shouting until I died of cold.

I do not want to go on being a root in the dark,
hesitating, stretched out, shivering with dreams,
downward, in the wet tripe of the earth,
soaking it up and thinking, eating every day.

I do not want to be the inheritor of so many misfortunes.
I do not want to continue as a root and as a tomb,
as a solitary tunnel, as a cellar full of corpses,
stiff with cold, dying with pain.

For this reason Monday burns like oil
at the sight of me arriving with my jail-face,
and it howls in passing like a wounded wheel,
and walks like hot blood toward nightfall.

And it shoves me along to certain corners, to certain damp houses,
to hospitals where the bones stick out of the windows,
to certain cobblers' shops smelling of vinegar,
to streets horrendous as crevices.

There are birds the color of sulfur, and horrible intestines
hanging from the doors of the houses that I hate,
there are forgotten sets of teeth in a coffeepot,
there are mirrors
that should have wept with shame and horror,
there are umbrellas all over the place, and poisons, and navels.

I stride along with calm, with eyes, with shoes,
with fury, with forgetfulness,
I pass, I cross offices and stores full of orthopedic appliances,
and courtyards hung with clothes hanging from a wire:
underpants, towels, and shirts which weep
show dirty tears.

1959

WIDOWER'S TANGO

Oh Maligna, by now you will have found the letter, by now you will
        have cried with rage
and you will have insulted the memory of my mother
calling her a rotten bitch and a mother of dogs,
by now you will have drunk alone, all by yourself, your afternoon tea
with your eyes on my old shoes which are empty forever,
and by now you will not be able to recall my illnesses, my dreams at
        night, my meals

without cursing me out loud as though I were still there,
complaining of the tropics, of the *coolies corringhis*,
of the poisonous fevers that were so hard on me,
and of the horrendous English whom I still hate.

Maligna, the truth of it, how huge the night is, how lonely the earth!
I have gone back again to single bedrooms,
to cold lunches in restaurants, and I
drop my pants and my shirts on the floor as I used to,
there are no hangers in my room, and nobody's pictures are on the walls.
How much of the shadow that is in my soul I would give to have you back;
the names of the months sound to me like threats
and the word *winter* is like the sound of a lugubrious drum.

Later on you will find buried near the coconut tree
the knife that I hid there for fear you would kill me,
and now suddenly I would be glad to smell its kitchen steel
used to the weight of your hand and the luster of your foot:
under the dampness of the ground, among the deaf roots,
in all the languages of men only the poor will know your name,
and the dense earth does not understand your name
made of impenetrable divine substances.

Thus it hurts me to think of the clear day of your legs
in repose like waters of the sun made to stay in place,
and the swallow that lives in your eyes sleeping and flying,
and the mad dog that you harbor in your heart,
and thus also I see the dead who are between us and will be from now on,
and I breathe ash and utter ruin in the air itself,
and the vast solitary space that will be around me forever.

I would give this wind off the giant sea for your hoarse breathing
heard in the long nights unmixed with oblivion,
becoming part of the atmosphere as the whip becomes part of the
      horse's skin.
And to hear you make water, in the darkness, at the bottom of the house,

as though you were pouring a slow, tremulous, silvery, obstinate honey,
how many times over would I yield up this choir of shadows that I possess,
and the clash of useless swords that is audible in my soul,
and the dove of blood, along on my forehead,
calling to things that have vanished, to beings who have vanished,
to substances incomprehensibly inseparable and lost.

1959

DEATH ALONE

There are cemeteries all by themselves,
tombs full of soundless bones,
the heart going through a tunnel,
in darkness, in darkness, in darkness,
we die inward like a shipwreck,
like a strangling of the heart,
like falling away from the skin of the soul.

There are cadavers,
there are cold sticky slabs that are feet,
there is death in the bones
like a pure sound,
like a barking without a dog,
coming from certain fields, from certain tombs,
growing in the darkness like a lament or the rain.

Sometimes when I am alone I see
coffins with sails
weigh anchor with pale corpses aboard, women with dead braids,
bakers white as angels,
pensive girls married to notaries,
coffins ascending the vertical river of the dead,
the purple river,
toward the source, their sails filled with the sound of death,
filled with the silent sound of death.

Death comes to the sonorous
like a shoe without a foot, like a suit without a man,
it comes to knock with a ring without a stone and without a finger,
it comes to shout without a mouth, without a tongue, without a throat.

Nevertheless its footsteps resound
and its garments resound, silently, like a tree.

I do not know, I have little learning, I can scarcely see,
but I believe that its song is the color of moist violets,
of violets that are used to the earth,
for the face of death is green,
and the glance of death is green,
with the sharp moisture of a violet leaf
and its grave color of exasperated winter.

But death goes through the world also dressed as a broom,
it licks the ground looking for the dead,
death is in the broom,
it is the tongue of death looking for the dead,
it is the needle of death looking for the thread.

Death is in the little beds,
in the slow mattresses, in the black blankets,
it lives stretched out, and suddenly it breathes:
it breathes a dark sound that fills the sheets,
and there are beds navigating in a harbor
where death is waiting, dressed as an admiral.

1959

ODE WITH A LAMENT

Oh girl among the roses, oh pressure of doves,
oh garrison of fish and rosebushes,
your soul is a bottle full of dry salt
and a bell full of grapes is your skin.

What a pity that I have nothing to give you except
the nails of my fingers, or eyelashes, or pianos melted by love,
or dreams which pour from my heart in torrents,
dreams covered with dust, which gallop like black riders,
dreams full of velocities and misfortunes.

I can love you only with kisses and poppies,
with garlands wet with rain,
my eyes full of ash-colored horses and yellow dogs.
I can love you only with waves on the shoulder,
amid random blows of sulfur, and waters lost in thought,
swimming against the cemeteries that run in certain rivers
with wet grass growing over the sad plaster tombs,
swimming across the sunken hearts
and the small pale pages of unburied children.

There is a great deal of death, there are funeral events
in my helpless passions and desolate kisses,
there is the water which falls in my head,
while my hair grows,
a water like time, a black unchained water,
with a nocturnal voice, with the cry
of a bird in the rain, with an unending
shadow, a shadow of a wet wing that protects my bones:
while I'm plain to be seen, while
I stare at myself endlessly in the mirrors and windowpanes,
I hear someone following me, calling me, sobbing,
with a sad voice rotted by time.

You are standing over the earth, full
of teeth and lightning.
You propagate kisses and you kill the ants.
You weep tears of health, of the onion, of the bee,
of the burning alphabet.
You are like a sword, blue and green,
and you undulate to the touch like a river.

Come to my soul dressed in white, with a branch
of bleeding roses and goblets of ashes,
come with an apple and a horse,
for there is a dark room with a broken candelabrum,
a few twisted chairs waiting for winter,
and a dead dove, with a number.

1959

AUTUMN RETURNS

A day dressed in mourning falls from the bells
like a fluttering veil of a roving widow,
it is a color, a dream
of cherries sunk in the earth,
a tail of smoke restlessly arriving
to change the color of water and of kisses.

I am not sure that it understands me: when night
approaches from the heights, when the solitary poet
at his window hears the galloping horse of autumn
and the trampled leaves of fear rustle in his arteries,
there is something over the sky, like the tongue of an ox,
thick, something uncertain in the sky and the atmosphere.

Things return to their place,
the indispensable lawyer, the hands, the oil,

the bottles,
all the signs of life: the beds, above all,
are filled with a bloody liquid,
the people deposit their secrets in sordid ears,
the assassins come down stairs,
but it's not that, but the old gallop,
the horse of old autumn, which trembles and endures.

The horse of old autumn has a red beard
and the froth of fear covers his cheeks
and the air that follows him is shaped like an ocean
and smells of vague buried decay.

Every day a color like ashes drops from the sky;
the doves must divide it for the earth:
the rope which is woven by oblivion and tears,
time which has slept long years in the bells,
everything,
the worn-out clothes, the women watching the snow fall,
the black poppies that no one can look at without dying,
everything falls into the hands that I raise
into the midst of the rain.

1959

WALTZ

I touch hatred like a daily breast;
I without ceasing come from garment to garment,
sleeping at a distance.

I am not, I do not serve, I do not know
anyone; I have no weapons of ocean or wood,
I do not live in this house.

My mouth is full of night and water.
The abiding moon determines
what I do not have.

What I have is in the midst of the waves.
A ray of water, a day for myself,
an iron depth.

There is no cross-tide, there is no shield, and no costume,
there is no special solution too deep to be sounded,
no vicious eyelid.

I live suddenly and other times I follow.
I touch a face suddenly and murder myself.
I have no time.

Do not look for me then running over
the usual wild thread or the
bleeding net.

Do not call me: that is my occupation.
Do not ask my name or my condition.
Leave me in the middle of my own moon
in my wounded ground.

1959

THEY COME FOR THE ISLANDS (1493)

The butchers laid waste the islands.
Guanahani was the first
in that history of torments.
The children of clay saw their
smiles smashed, battered
their stance slight as deers',

all the way to death they did not understand.
They were trussed up and tortured,
they were lit and burned
they were gnawed and buried.
And when time danced around again
waltzing among the palms
the green hall was empty.

      Nothing was left but bones
      rigidly fastened
      in the form of a cross, to the greater
      glory of God and of men.

      From the chief claypits
      and green boughs of Sotavento
      to the coral cays
      the knife of Narvaez went carving.
      Here the cross, here the rosary,
      here the Virgin of the Stake.
      Glowing Cuba, Columbus's jewel,
      received the standard and the knees
      in its wet sand.

                1968

Nicanor Parra | Spanish
born 1914

MEMORIES OF YOUTH

All I'm sure of is that I kept going back and forth,
Sometimes I bumped into trees,
Bumped into beggars,
I forced my way through a thicket of chairs and tables,
With my soul on a thread I watched the great leaves fall.
But the whole thing was useless,
At every turn I sank deeper into a sort of jelly;
People laughed at my fits,
The characters stirred in their armchairs like seaweed moved by the waves
And women gave me horrid looks
Dragging me up, dragging me down,
Making me cry and laugh against my will.

All this evoked in me a feeling of nausea
And a storm of incoherent sentences,
Threats, insults, pointless curses,
Also certain exhausting pelvic motions,
Macabre dances, that left me
Short of breath
Unable to raise my head for days,
For nights.

I kept going back and forth, that's true,
My soul drifted through the streets
Calling for help, begging for a little tenderness,
With pencil and paper I went into cemeteries
Determined not to be fooled.
I went round and round the same fact,
I studied everything in minute detail
Or I tore out my hair in a tantrum.

And in this state I began my classroom career.
I heaved myself around literary gatherings like a man with a bullet wound.
Crossing the thresholds of private houses,
With my sharp tongue I tried to get the spectators to understand me,
They went on reading the paper
Or disappeared behind a taxi.
Then where could I go!
At that hour the shops were shut;
I thought of a slice of onion I'd seen during dinner
And of the abyss that separates us from the other abysses.

1965

THE TUNNEL

In my youth I lived for a time in the house of some aunts
On the heels of the death of a gentleman with whom they had been
      intimately connected
Whose ghost tormented them without pity
Making life intolerable for them.

At the beginning I ignored their telegrams
And their letters composed in the language of another day,
Larded with mythological allusions
And proper names that meant nothing to me
Some referring to sages of antiquity
Or minor medieval philosophers
Or merely to neighbors of theirs.

To give up the university just like that
And break off the joys of a life of pleasure,
To put a stop to it all
In order to placate the caprices of three hysterical old women
Riddled with every kind of personal difficulty,
This, to a person of my character, seemed
An uninspiring prospect,
A brainless idea.

Four years, just the same, I lived in The Tunnel
In the company of those frightening old ladies,
Four years of uninterrupted torture
Morning, noon, and night.
The delightful hours that I had spent under the trees
Were duly replaced by weeks of revulsion,
Months of anguish, which I did my best to disguise
For fear of attracting their curiosity.
They stretched into years of ruin and misery.
For centuries my soul was imprisoned
In a bottle of drinking water!

My spiritualist conception of the world
Left me obviously inferior to every fact I was faced with:
I saw everything through a prism
In the depths of which the images of my aunts intertwined like
        living threads
Forming a sort of impenetrable chain mail
Which hurt my eyes making them more and more useless.

A young man of scanty means can't size things up.
He lives in a bell jar called Art
Or Pleasure or Science
Trying to make contact with a world of relationships
That exist only for him and a small group of friends.

Under the influence of a sort of water vapor
That found its way through the floor of the room
Flooding the atmosphere till it blotted out everything
I spent the nights at my work table
Absorbed in practicing automatic writing.

But why rake deeper into this wretched affair?
Those old women led me on disgracefully
With their false promises, with their weird fantasies,
With their cleverly performed sufferings.
They managed to keep me enmeshed for years

Making me feel obliged to work for them, though it was never said:
Agricultural labors,
Purchase and sale of cattle,
Until one night, looking through the keyhole
I noticed that one of my aunts—
The paralytic!—
Was getting about beautifully on the tips of her toes,
And I came to, knowing I'd been bewitched.

1965

THE VIPER

For years I was doomed to worship a contemptible woman,
Sacrifice myself for her, endure endless humiliations and sneers,
Work night and day to feed her and clothe her,
Perform several crimes, commit several misdemeanors,
Practice petty burglary by moonlight,
Forge compromising documents,
For fear of a scornful glance from her bewitching eyes.
During brief phases of understanding we used to meet in parks
And have ourselves photographed together driving a motorboat,
Or we would go to a nightclub
And fling ourselves into an orgy of dancing
That went on until well after dawn.
For years I was under the spell of that woman.
She used to appear in my office completely naked
And perform contortions that defy the imagination,
Simply to draw my poor soul into her orbit
And above all to wring from me my last penny.
She absolutely forbade me to have anything to do with my family.
To get rid of my friends this viper made free with defamatory libels
That she published in a newspaper she owned.
Passionate to the point of delirium, she never let up for an instant,
Commanding me to kiss her on the mouth
And to reply at once to her silly questions
Concerning, among other things, eternity and the afterlife,

Subjects that upset me terribly,
Producing buzzing in my ears, recurrent nausea, sudden fainting spells,
Which she turned to account with that practical turn of mind that
    distinguished her,
Putting her clothes on without wasting a moment
And clearing out of my apartment, leaving me flat.

This situation dragged on for five years and more.
There were periods when we lived together in a round room
In a plush district near the cemetery, sharing the rent.
(Some nights we had to interrupt our honeymoon
To cope with the rats that streamed in through the window.)

The viper kept a meticulous account book
In which she noted every penny I borrowed from her,
She would not let me use the toothbrush I had given her myself,
And she accused me of having ruined her youth:
With her eyes flashing fire she threatened to take me to court
And make me pay part of the debt within a reasonable period
Since she needed the money to go on with her studies.
Then I had to take to the street and live on public charity,
Sleeping on park benches
Where the police found me time and again, dying,
Among the first leaves of autumn.
Fortunately that state of affairs went no further,
For one time—and again I was in a park,
Posing for a photographer—
A pair of delicious feminine hands suddenly covered my eyes
While a voice that I loved asked me who am I.
You are my love, I answered serenely.
My angel! she said nervously.
Let me sit on your knees once again!
It was then that I was able to ponder the fact that she was now wearing
    brief tights.
It was a memorable meeting, though full of discordant notes.
I have bought a plot of land not far from the slaughterhouse,
    she exclaimed.

I plan to build a sort of pyramid there
Where we can spend the rest of our days.
I have finished my studies, I have been accepted to the bar,
I have a tidy bit of capital at my disposal;
Let's go into some lucrative business, we two, my love, she added,
Let's build our nest far from the world.
Enough of your foolishness, I answered, I have no confidence in
        your plans.
Bear in mind that my real wife
Can at any moment leave both of us in the most frightful poverty.
My children are grown up, time has elapsed,
I feel utterly exhausted, let me have a minute's rest,
Give me a little water, woman,
Get me something to eat from somewhere,
I'm starving,
I can't work for you any more,
It's all over between us.

1965

THE TRAP

During that time I kept out of circumstances that were too full of mystery
As people with stomach ailments avoid heavy meals,
I preferred to stay at home inquiring into certain questions
Concerning the propagation of spiders,
To which end I would shut myself up in the garden
And not show myself in public until late at night;
Or else, in shirtsleeves, defiant,
I would hurl angry glances at the moon,
Trying to get rid of those bilious fancies
That cling like polyps to the human soul.
When I was alone I was completely self-possessed,
I went back and forth fully conscious of my actions
Or I would stretch out among the planks of the cellar

And dream, think up ways and means, resolve little emergency problems.
It was at that moment that I put into practice my famous method for
      interpreting dreams
Which consists in doing violence to myself and then imagining what I
      would like,
Conjuring up scenes that I had worked out beforehand with the help of
      powers from other worlds.
In this manner I was able to obtain priceless information
Concerning a string of anxieties that afflict our being:
Foreign travel, erotic disorders, religious complexes.
But all precautions were inadequate,
Because, for reasons hard to set forth
I began sliding automatically down a sort of inclined plane.
My soul lost altitude like a punctured balloon,
The instinct of self-preservation stopped functioning
And, deprived of my most essential prejudices,
I fell unavoidably into the telephone trap
Which sucks in everything around it, like a vacuum,
And with trembling hands I dialed that accursed number
Which even now I repeat automatically in my sleep.
Uncertainty and misery filled the seconds that followed,
While I, like a skeleton standing before that table from hell
Covered with yellow cretonne,
Waited for an answer from the other end of the world,
The other half of my being, imprisoned in a pit.
Those intermittent telephone noises
Worked on me like a dentist's drill,
They sank into my soul like needles shot from the sky
Until, when the moment itself arrived
I started to sweat and to stammer feverishly,
My tongue like a veal steak
Obtruded between my being and her who was listening,
Like those black curtains that separate us from the dead.
I never wanted to conduct those over-intimate conversations
Which I myself provoked, just the same, in my stupid way,
My voice thick with desire, and electrically charged.

Hearing myself called by my first name
In that tone of forced familiarity
Filled me with a vague discomfort,
With anguished localized disturbances which I contrived to keep in check
With a hurried system of questions and answers
Which roused in her a state of pseudoerotic effervescence
That eventually affected me as well
With incipient erections and a feeling of doom.
Then I'd make myself laugh and as a result fall into a state of
        mental prostration.
Those ridiculous little chats went on for hours
Until the lady who ran the pension appeared behind the screen
Brutally breaking off our stupid idyll.
Those contortions of a petitioner at the gates of heaven
And those catastrophes that so wore down my spirit
Did not stop altogether when I hung up
For usually we had agreed
To meet next day in a soda fountain
Or at the door of a church whose name I prefer to forget.

1965

ON THIS EARTH

What kills me
is my
chest.

(Chest
shaped like
Spain.)

Get lots of air, the doctor
told me, lots of ai—

—Okay, where?

1959

Claudio Rodriguez | Spanish
1934–1999

MY FRIEND ALWAYS...

Not he who in spring goes out to the field
and loses himself in the blue festivities
of men whom he loves, and is blind to the old
leather beneath the fresh down, shall be my friend always

but you, true friendship, celestial pedestrian, who in winter
leave your house in the breaking dawn and set out
on foot, and in our cold find eternal shelter
and in our deep drought the voice of the harvests.

1958

Agostinho Neto

Portuguese
Angola
1922-1979

KINAXIXI

I liked to sit down
on a bench in Kinaxixi
at six o'clock of a hot evening
and just sit there...

Someone would come
maybe
to sit beside me

And I would see the black faces of the people
going uptown
in no hurry
expressing absence in the jumbled Kimbundu
they conversed in.

I would see the tired footsteps
of the servants whose fathers are also servants
looking for love here, glory there, wanting
something more than drunkenness in every alcohol

Neither happiness nor hate

After the sun had set
lights would be turned on and I
would wander off
thinking that our life after all is simple
too simple
for anyone who is tired and still has to walk.

1962

NIGHT

I live
in the dark quarters of the world
without light or life.

Anxious to live,
I walk in the streets
feeling my way,
leaning into my shapeless dreams,
stumbling into servitude.

——Dark quarters,
     worlds of misery

where the will is watered down
and men
are confused with things.

I walk, lurching
through the unlit
unknown streets crowded
with mystery and terror,
I, arm in arm with ghosts.

And the night too is dark.

1962

FRIEND MUSSUNDA

Here I am,
friend Mussunda,
        here I am,

with you.
With the established victory of your joy
and of your conscience.

    ——*you whom the god of death has made!*
        you whom the god of death has made, made... *

Remember?

The sadness of those days
when we were there
with mangoes to eat,
bemoaning our fate
and the women of Funda,
our songs of lamentation,
our despairs,
the clouds in our eyes,
Remember?

Here I am,
friend Mussunda.
To you
I owe my life,
to the same devotion, the same love
with which you saved me
from the constrictor's embrace

to your strength
which transforms the fates of men.

To you,
friend Mussunda, I owe my life to you.

———

*These two lines, in the native language of Angola, are part of a children's chant.

And I write
poems you don't understand!
Can you imagine my anguish?

Here I am,
friend Mussunda,
writing poems you don't understand.

It wasn't this
that we wanted, I know that,
but in the mind, in the intelligence,
that's where we're alive.

We're alive,
friend Mussunda,
we're alive!

Inseparable
still on the road to our vision.

The hearts beat
rhythms of foggy nights,
the feet dance

the sounds do not die in our ears

    ——*you whom the god of death has made...*

We're alive!

1962

Michelangelo | Italian 1475-1564

TO POPE JULIUS II

Sir if one of the old proverbs
is true it's *He who can will not*
You have been taken in by little stories
words
and have rewarded the enemies of truth

I was faithful to you long ago and have not changed
As rays are given to the sun I gave you
myself
but my days are nothing to you
never touch you
the more I try the less I delight you

Once I hoped to be raised by your eminence
know your massive justice and the might of your sword
when I needed them
not the voice of echo

But heaven itself mocks any virtue that looks
for a place in the world
sending it to pick fruit from a dry tree

1967

Joachim du Bellay
French
1522–1560

Happy the man who like Ulysses
    has made a good voyage or like him who seized
    the fleece and then came back knowing and wise
    to spend among his kin the rest of his days

Alas when will I see smoke from the chimneys
    of my little village and in what season look
    on the walled garden of my simple house
    that is a province and much more to me

I would rather have the roof my fathers made
    than the proud fronts of Roman palaces
    and thin slate rather than their hard marble

rather the Gaulish Loire than Latin Tiber
    my little hill than the Mount Palatine
    the sweetness of Anjou than the wind from the sea

1967

Jean Antoine de Baïf | French
1532–1589

DEDICATION OF A MIRROR

I that for letting a smile's favor
Loose from my youth in a light hour
Would with suitors' press and fervor
Find my doorway darkened over
Now to Venus for her to keep
The promised mirror tender up,
For the shape which of late I wear
Is such as will not bear review
And the face once this surface knew
Stirs no such shadows any more.

1948

François de Malherbe   French
                            1558-1628

INSCRIPTION FOR A FOUNTAIN

Passerby, see how this water
Wells up and away is whirled:
Thus flows the glory of the world.
Only God remains forever.

1958

Michel-Jean Sedaine

French
1719-1797
song published in 1784

I'D RATHER DRINK

Let Saladin the emperor
In his garden bring together
A whole flock of damsels, all
Young and all delectable,
For his after-breakfast pleasure;
    Never mind, never mind,
That's quite harmless, to my mind;
I'm like Gregory: I think
    I'd rather drink.

Let a lord or lofty noble
Pawn the tower of his castle
To depart for the Crusade,
Let him leave his lady bride
In the hands of worthy people;
    Never mind, never mind,
That's quite harmless, to my mind;
I'm like Gregory: I think
    I'd rather drink.

Let Richard, when his courage calls,
Brave a multitude of perils
So that, far from England, he
May subdue another country
Full of heathen infidels;
    Never mind, never mind,
That's quite harmless, to my mind;
I'm like Gregory: I think
    I'd rather drink.

1957

Alexandre Duval | French
1767-1842
song published in 1821

ROMANCE OF JOSEPH

Fourteen years I knew at most,
Scarcely from infancy removed,
When I followed in my trust
Those wicked brothers whom I loved.
Our numerous flocks we left to graze
Upon green Sichem's pasturelands.
Still simple as a child I was,
And timid even as my lambs.

Close by three palms that stood alone
Unto the Lord I said my prayer,
When, by those wicked brothers taken...
I tremble even now with fear!
Into a damp and cold abyss
They thrust me down with angry force,
While I against their crime oppose
Only my innocence and tears.

Alas, when I was near to die
They brought me forth out of that grave.
To merchants from Arabia
They tendered me, to be a slave.
While they the price paid for their brother
Counted, and shared out the gold,
I, alas, wept for my father
And the ingrates who had me sold.

1957

Tristan Corbière | French
1845-1875

LETTER FROM MEXICO

Vera Cruz, February 10

You gave me the boy to look after.—He's dead.
And more than one of his mates too, poor dear creature.
The crew… there's no crew any more. Maybe one or
    Two of us will get back. That's the luck of it.

Nothing's as grand as that: a Sailor—ask any man;
What they all want to be, on land—That's sure enough.
Without the discomfort. And it's nothing else: look what a tough
    Apprenticeship, and he's only begun!

I cry writing it down, I, old *Weather-Eyes*.
I'd have given my own skin, yes I would, like that,
To send him back to you… It's not my fault. It's not.
    It makes no sense, that sickness.

The fever strikes like bells here. We'll all be
Drawing our rations in the cemetery.
The zouave calls it—he's from Paris, that one—
    "The garden of acclimatization."

Console yourself. They're all dying like flies. I found
A couple of things in his bag, keepsakes: a picture
Of a girl, and a pair of slippers, small size, and
    Marked: *Present for my sister.*

He said tell his mamma he said his prayer.
Tell his father he would rather have fallen
In a battle. Two angels were with him at the end.
    A sailor. An old soldier.

1958

PARIS AT NIGHT

It is not a city, it is a world.

—It is the sea—flat calm—and the spring tide,
With the thunderings far out, has departed.
It will be back, the swell, in its own sound rolling.
—Listen to that: the crabs of night at their scratching…

—It is the dry bed of the Styx: Diogenes,
That rag-man, lantern in hand, calm as you please,
Passes. By the black stream perverted poets
Fish, using their empty skulls for worm-pots.

—It is the field: a flight of hideous harpies,
Wheeling, pounces to glean scabby bandages;
The gutter-rabbit, out after rats, keeps wide
Of Bondy's boys, who tread their grapes by night.

—It is death: the police sleep.—Above, love
Has her siesta, sucking the meat of a heavy
Arm where the dead kiss raises its red sign…
The single hour.—Listen: not a dream moving.

—It is life: listen: the living spring sings
The everlasting song on the slobbering
Head of a sea-god stretching his green limbs and naked
On a morgue slab, with his eyes open wide.

1958

Guillaume Apollinaire | French
1880–1918

THE MIRABEAU BRIDGE

Under the Mirabeau Bridge the Seine
                        Flows and our love
                    Must I be reminded again
How joy came always after pain

            Night comes the hour is rung
            The days go I remain

Hands within hands we stand face to face
                        While underneath
                    The bridge of our arms passes
The loose wave of our gazing which is endless

            Night comes the hour is rung
            The days go I remain

Love slips away like this water flowing
                        Love slips away
                    How slow life is in its going
And hope is so violent a thing

            Night comes the hour is rung
            The days go I remain

The days pass the weeks pass and are gone
                        Neither time that is gone
                    Nor love ever returns again
Under the Mirabeau Bridge flows the Seine

Night comes the hour is rung
The days go I remain

1956

AUTUMN

A bowlegged peasant and his ox receding
Through the mist slowly through the mist of autumn
Which hides the shabby and sordid villages

And out there as he goes the peasant is singing
A song of love and infidelity
About a ring and a heart that someone is breaking

Oh the autumn the autumn has been the death of summer
In the mist there are two gray shapes receding

1956

STAR

I think of Gaspard that certainly was not
His real name he is travelling he has left the town
Of Blue Lanchi where all the children called him papa
At the foot of the calm gulf facing the seven islands
Gaspard walks on and longs for the rice and the tea
        The Milky Way
At night since naturally he is walking
Only at night often catches his eye
        But Gaspard
Knows full well that one must not follow it

1956

Jules Supervielle | French
1884–1960

THE TIP OF THE FLAME

All through his life
He had liked to read
By a candle
And often he passed
His hand over the flame
To convince himself
That he was alive,
That he was alive.

Since the day he died
He has kept beside him
A lighted candle
But he hides his hands.

1960

Henri Michaux | French
1899-1984

REPOSE IN CALAMITY

Calamity, my great laborer,
Sit down, Calamity,
Take it easy,
Let's take it easy for a minute, both of us,
Easy.
You find me, you get the hang of me, you try me out,
I'm the ruin of you.

My big theater, my harbor, my hearth,
My golden cave,
My future, my real mother, my horizon,
In your light, in your great spaces, in your horror,
I let myself go.

1962

MY LIFE

You go off without me, my life,
You roll,
And me, I'm still waiting to take the first step.
You take the battle somewhere else,
Deserting me.
I've never followed you.

I can't really make out anything in your offers.
The little I want, you never bring it.
I miss it; that's why I lay claim to so much.
To so many things, to infinity almost...
Because of that little bit that's missing, that you never bring.

1962

Jean Follain | French
1903–1971

SIGNS

Sometimes when a customer in a shadowy restaurant
is shelling an almond
a hand comes to rest on his narrow shoulder
he hesitates to finish his glass
the forest in the distance is resting under its snows
the sturdy waitress has turned pale
he will have to let the winter night fall
has she not often seen
on the last page
of a book of modest learning
the word *end* printed
in ornate capitals?

1960

THE PLATE

When the serving girl's hands
drop the pale round plate
the color of clouds
the pieces have to be picked up
while the light trembles overhead
in the masters' dining room
and the old school stammers
an uncertain mythology
in which one hears the names
when the wind stops
of all the false gods.

1967

EVE

One book has it that Eve
came from the *haya* root
meaning to live
meanwhile creatures
sure of their existence
pass on to girls knowledge
of human passions
but the youngest
holds a blond apple
on a worn sill
and does nothing else
before she goes to sleep.

1967

EXILE

In the evening they listen to the same
music no one could call merry
a face appears at a corner
of the inhabited world
the roses open
a bell has rung under the clouds
in front of the pillared doorway.
A seated man says to all comers
in his gray velvet
showing his furrowed hands
as long as I live no one
touches my dogs my friends.

1967

IMPERIAL HAMLET

In the hamlet in the rye fields
they still preserve an air
that invites ceremony
the doors stand open.
The word *liberty*
engraved in a stone
is reflected in a broken mirror.
The roots of a tree
stand out of the scuffed ground.
One of the houses
has two lamps
someone who lives there is putting on
a garment lined with scarlet
from the days of his youth.

1967

SOLITARIES

Their doors always open badly
behind them the fire-colored
animal is asleep
they know whoever passes
on the curving road
man or woman just by the footstep
they watch for a moment
the ornate lamp
hanging from the black ceiling
a spotted green plant is dying
a lost child cries
under the vast low sky
then at last it snows.

1967

WORLD'S END

At the world's end
on worn-out ground
the one talks of the flowers
adorning Argonne china
in their red pigment is mixed
the gold of old Dutch ducats
dissolved in aqua regia.
How soon the night falls
the other answers
times goes so fast
in this empty country.

1967

Anne-Marie Kegels | French
1912–1994

NOCTURNAL HEART

Master of blood I am yours.
O tireless captain
upright on the plains of sand,
at night, at night I hear you
march toward a doubtful sea
with footsteps falsely restrained
—at that time I touch my breath,
I search for you with my bare wrist,
I defend you against the seaweed,
the salt, the wakened fish,
we faint under a wave,
people tell of two that are drowned,
of a fog mowing the beach.

Midnight descends, covers my lips,
keeps me from calling for help.
We float, forgotten by day.

1961

Pierre Delisle | French born 1908

Consider for a moment
The wakening of the minerals
To their omnipotence
When they will come
At night into the villages
And ambush the squeals of the unweaned
And steal their names.

1967

Voice closed like a lamp
The mother of memory
Says:

I give you my daughter
I give you memory

You will both be lost
You will both be absent

As long as she lives with you.

1967

I love to speak in a low voice of the seasons of suffering.
They are she-asses travelling on the mountain
Looking for oblivion.

Children climb on their backs as they are seen to do in the parks of
    great houses
Then we stand for a long time with our chests against the grille
Our eyes become the past.

1967

Philippe Jaccottet | French
born 1925

A sowing of tears
on the changed face,
the glittering season
of rivers gone wild:
grief that hollows the earth

Age watches the snow
receding on the mountains

1967

DAWN

Hour when the moon mists over
at the approach of a mouth
murmuring a hidden name

so that one can scarcely make out
the comb and the hair

1967

Gottfried Keller | German
1819–1890

Every wing in the world had fallen.
The white snow lay still, glittering.
No cloud hung in the stars' pavilion.
No wave hammered the hard lake.

The lake's tree came up out of the depths
Till its top froze in the ice.
The lake spirit climbed up the branches
And looked hard through the green ice, upward.

I stood on the thin glass there
That divided the black depths from me;
I saw, limb by limb, her beauty
Pressed close under my feet.

Through muffled sobbing her hands
Played over the hard lid.
I have not forgotten that lightless face;
It rises in my mind without end, without end.

1967

Friedrich Nietzsche | German 1844-1900

AT THE CASTING OF THE THIRD SKIN

Now the skin on me warps and splits
and already the snake in me
has digested so much earth that it craves
for earth with a new heaving
and I crawl between stone and grass
hungering on my crooked way
to eat what I always ate you you
provender of snakes O earth

1967

AGAINST THE LAWS

Starting now the hours of the clock
will hang on a hair around my neck
starting now the stars will stop
in their courses sun cock-crow shadows
and everything that time proclaimed
is now deaf and dumb and blind
for me all nature is silenced
with the ticking of the law and its measure

1967

Ernst Stadler | German 1883-1914

My heart is standing up to its throat in yellow harvest light
    like land ripe for mowing under summer heavens.
Soon the song of the sickles will be ringing through the plain;
    my blood listens in the noon heat, sunk in happiness.
Granaries of my life, long desolate,
    all your gates will stand open like sluices;
the golden flood of sheaves will move on your floors like
    the sea.

1967

Gottfried Benn | German
1886–1956

Look: the stars, the fangs
of light, and heaven and the sea,
what herdsmen's songs they
drive fading before them,
and you also who have summoned
voices and thought out your circle
follow the messenger
of night down the hushed steps.

Once you have emptied
the myths and the words, you must go,
you will not see again
a new company of gods,
their Euphrates thrones,
their writing, their wall—
pour, Myrmidon,
the dark wine on the land.

However the hours were welcomed,
anguish and tears of being,
everything blooms in the flowing
of this wine of night,
the aeon streams out in silence,
the shores have almost gone—
give back to the messenger
the crown, the dream, the gods.

1967

Johannes Bobrowski

German
1917-1965

THE NIGHT FISHER

In the beautiful foliage
the silence
unconsoled.
Light
with the hands
above a wall.
The sand flows from roots.
Sand
flow red in the water
far from here, follow
voices, make your way in the dark,
in the morning lay out your booty.
The voices pale as silver
sing.
Carry off to safety
in the beautiful foliage
the ears,
the voices sing: what
is dead is dead.

1967, translated with
Jean-Pierre Hammer

Fedor Tyutchev

Russian
1803–1873

CICERO

When the state tore at itself in agony
Rome's orator said, "I got up
too late and the night of Rome overtook me
on the way." Maybe,
but as you bade farewell to Rome's glory
you beheld from the Capitoline Hill
her bloody star
setting in full majesty.

Blessèd is he
whose visit to the world has fallen
in its moments of destiny.
The kind powers have welcomed him
to their banquet, to converse as an equal. He
sees the striding glories that they see,
he has a place at their councils, he drinks
from their own cup immortality,
in his time he lives as they do in heaven.

1968, translated with Olga Carlisle

Alexander Blok

Russian
1880–1921

TO ZINAIDA GIPPIUS

Those born in backwater years
forget their own way. Russia
gave birth to us in her years of anguish
and we can forget nothing.

Years of holocaust, do you
herald madness, or the advent of hope?
Days of war, days of freedom,
have stained our faces with bloody light.

We are speechless. The bells'
alarms sealed our lips. Where there was
a burning in our hearts once
there is nothing now, fixed, like a death.

Over the bed where we are dying
let the hoarse ravens sail—
may others, more worthy, O God, O God,
gaze on Thy kingdom!

1968, translated with Olga Carlisle

SELECTED TRANSLATIONS 1948–1968 *141*

Sergey Esenin

Russian
1895–1925

Wind whistles through the steep fence
      hides in the grass
a drunk and a thief
      I'll end my days
the light sinking in red hills
      shows me the path
I'm not the only one on it
      not the only one
plowed Russia stretches away
      grass and then snow
no matter what part I'd come from
      our cross is the same
I believe in my secret hour
      as in ikons not painted by hands
like a tramp who sleeps back of a fence
      it will rise my inviolate savior
but through the blue tattered fogs
      of unhallowed rivers
I may pass with a drunken smile
      never knowing him
no tear lighting up on my lashes
      to break my dream
joy like a blue dove
      dropping into the dark
sadness resuming
      its vindictive song
but may the wind of my grave
      dance like a peasant in spring

1967, translated with Olga Carlisle

In the country of yellow nettles
          the twig fences are brittle
the log houses huddle like orphans
          into the pussy willows

through fields over the hills' blue
          by the greenness of lakes
a road of sand leads to the mountains
          of Siberia

Between Mongols and Finns Russia
          is lost there before she is frightened
along the road men make their way
          in irons

Each one has robbed or killed
          as his fate would have it
I am in love with the grief of their eyes
          and the graves in their cheeks

many have killed from pure joy
          they are simple-hearted
but in their darkened faces
          the blue mouths are twisted

I cherish one secret dream
          that I am pure in heart
but I too will cut a throat
          to the whistling of autumn

I too on the blown road
          on these same sands
will go with a rope at the neck
          to make love to mourning

I will smile as I go by
      I will swell out my chest
and the storm will lick over
      the way I came

1967, translated with Olga Carlisle

I am the last poet of the villages
the plank bridge lifts a plain song
I stand at a farewell service
birches swinging leaves like censers

The golden flame will burn down
in the candle of waxen flesh
and the moon a wooden clock
will caw caw my midnight

On the track in the blue field
soon the iron guest will appear
his black hand will seize
oats that the dawn sowed

In a lifeless and alien grip
my poems will die too
only nodding oats
will mourn for their old master

The wind will take up their neighing
they will all dance in the mourning
soon the moon on a wooden clock
will caw caw my midnight

1967, translated with Olga Carlisle

It's done. I've left the home fields.
       There'll be no going back.
The green wings all over the poplars
       will never ring again.

Without me the hunched house sinks lower.
       My old dog died long ago.
I know God means I'm to die
       among the bent streets of Moscow.

I like the city, in its old script,
       though it's grown fat with age.
The gold somnolence of Asia
       dozes on the cupolas.

But at night when the moon shines, shines,
       shines, the devil knows how,
I take a side street, head down,
       into the same tavern.

A lair full of din and roaring,
       but all night till daylight
I read out poems to whores
       and drink with cutthroats.

My heart beats faster and faster,
       I pick the wrong moments
to say, "I'm like you, I'm lost,
       I can never go back."

Without me the hunched house sinks lower.
       My old dog died long ago.
I know God means I'm to die
       among the bent streets of Moscow.

1967, translated with Olga Carlisle

Have you seen
running on the plain
on shoes of cast metal
the train hiding in the lake mists
blowing down its iron nostrils

and behind him
galloping over the high grasses
as though in the wild races at a fair
flinging his thin legs toward his chin the colt
with the red mane

the darling
the little idiot
where does he think he's running
Doesn't he know that all his kind
have lost to the steel cavalry
Doesn't he know there's no racing
in unnoticed fields that can bring back
the time when they'd trade
to the north of the Black Sea
for the right horse
two beautiful girls from the plain country
The fate of markets has troubled the face
of our still waters
waking them with the gnashing of iron Now
for a locomotive it would cost you tons
of the meat and skins of horses

1967, translated with Olga Carlisle

They are drinking here again brawling sobbing
to the amber woes of the accordion
they curse their luck and they hark back
to a Russia—a Moscow—of other days

For my part I duck my head
my eyes foundering in wine
rather than look fate in the face
I think of something else for a while

There is something that we have all lost forever
my dark blue May my pale blue June
that must be why the corpse smell
dogs this frantic carousal

Oh today's a great day for the Russians
the homemade vodka's flowing
and the noseless accordionist's singing
of the Volga and the secret police

They're grumbling that bony October
caught them all in its blizzard
courage has gone back to whetting
the knife from its boot

A hatred shifts in the eyes
rebellion grates in the raised voices
and they pity the young and foolish
whose blood flamed up and burned away

Where are you now and why so far
do we shine brightly for you
the accordionist's on a vodka cure
for his clap caught in the civil war

No the lost Russia will not be silenced
on all sides the rot feeds a wild courage—
oh Russia my Russia
rising in Asia

1967, translated with Olga Carlisle

Osip Mandelstam | Russian
1891–1938

I have forgotten the word I wanted to say.
A blind swallow returns to the palace of shadows
on clipped wings to flicker among the Transparent Ones.
In oblivion they are singing the night song.

No sound from the birds. No flowers on the immortelles.
The horses of night have transparent manes.
A little boat drifts on the dry river.
Among the crickets the word fades into oblivion.

And it rises slowly like a pavilion or a temple,
performs the madness of Antigone,
or falls at one's feet, a dead swallow,
with Stygian tenderness and a green branch.

Oh to bring back also the shyness of clairvoyant
fingers, the swelling joy of recognition.
I shrink from the wild grieving of the Muses,
from the mists, the ringing, the opening void.

It is given to mortals to love, to recognize,
to make sounds move to their fingers,
but I have forgotten what I wanted to say
and a bodiless thought returns to the palace of shadows.

The Transparent One still speaks, but of nothing.
Still a swallow, a friend known as a girl, Antigone.
The reverberations of Stygian remembrance
burn like black ice on one's lips.

dated "November 1920"

1967, translated with Olga Carlisle

When Psyche, who is Life, steps down into the shadows,
the translucent wood, following Persephone,
a blind swallow casts itself at her feet
with Stygian tenderness and a green branch.

The shades swarm to welcome the refugee,
their new little companion, and greet her with eager wailing,
wringing their frail arms before her
in awe and trouble and shy hope.

One of them holds out a mirror, and another, perfume,
because the soul is a woman and fond of trifles.
And the silence of the leafless forest is spotted
with transparent voices, dry laments, like a fine rain.

And in the fond confusion, uncertain where to begin,
the soul does not recognize the transparent woods.
She breathes on the mirror and she still clutches
the copper wafer, the fee for the misty crossing.

dated "1920"

1967, translated with Olga Carlisle

The thread of gold cordial flowed from the bottle
with such languor that the hostess found time to say
here in mournful Tauris where our fates have cast us
we are never bored—with a glance over her shoulder.

On all hands the rites of Bacchus, as though the whole world
held only guards and dogs. As you go you see no one.
And the placid days roll past like heavy barrels. Far off
in the ancient rooms there are voices. Can't make them out. Can't answer.

After tea we went out into the great brown garden.
Dark blinds are dropped like eyelashes on the windows.
We move along the white columns looking at grapes. Beyond them
airy glass has been poured over the drowsing mountains.

I said the grapevines live on like an antique battle,
with gnarled cavalry tangling in curving waves.
Here in stone-starred Tauris is an art of Hellas: here, rusted,
are the noble ranks of the golden acres.

Meanwhile silence stands in the white room like a spinning wheel,
smelling of vinegar, paint, wine cool from the cellar.
Do you remember in the Greek house the wife they all loved?
Not Helen. The other. And how long she embroidered?

Golden fleece, where are you then, golden fleece?
All the way the heaved weight of the sea rumbled.
Leaving his boat and its sea-wearied sails,
Odysseus returned, filled with space and time.

       dated "1917"

1967, translated with Olga Carlisle

    I could not keep your hands in my own,
    I failed the salt tender lips,
    so I must wait now for dawn in the timbered Acropolis.
    How I loathe the aging stockades and their tears.

    The Achaeans are constructing the horse in the dark,
    hacking out the sides with their dented saws.
    Nothing quiets the blood's dry fever, and for you
    there is no designation, no sound, no modelled likeness.

How did I dare to think you might come back?
Why did I tear myself from you before it was time?
The dark has not faded yet, nor the cock crowed,
nor the hot ax bitten wood.

Resin has seeped from the stockade like transparent tears
and the town is conscious of its own wooden ribs,
but blood has rushed to the stairs and started climbing
and in dreams three times men have seen the seductive image.

Where is Troy, the beloved? The royal, the queenly roof.
Priam's high bird house will be hurled down
while arrows rattle like dry rain
and grow from the ground like shoots of a hazel.

The pinprick of the last star vanishes without pain,
morning will tap at the shutter, a gray swallow,
and the slow day, like an ox that wakes on straw,
will lumber out from its long sleep to cross the rough haycocks.

dated "December 1920"

1967, translated with Olga Carlisle

Iosip Brodsky | Russian 1940-1996

THE BLIND MUSICIANS

The blind go their way
    by night.
It's easier to cross
the squares
    at night.
The blind live
feeling their way,
brushing the world with their hands,
knowing neither shadow nor light,
and their hands drift over the stones
built into walls
of men, women,
children,
    money,
walls that cannot be broken,
    better
to follow along them.
Against them the music
    hurls itself
and the stones soak it up.
In them the music dies
under the hands.
It's hard dying at night, hard
to die feeling your way.

The way of the blind is
simpler, the blind
    cross the empty squares.

1967, translated with
Wladimir Weidlé

THE VERBS

In the silence the verbs surround me
like faces of strangers,
                              the verbs,
famished verbs, naked verbs,
essential verbs, deaf verbs,
verbs with no names, mere verbs,
verbs that live in caves,
speak in caves,
are born in caves,
under the shifting levels
of the universal optimism.

They go to work every morning,
mix cement, haul stones,
build the city... No, they erect
a monument to their own solitude.
They recede as we disappear in the memory
of someone else, they keep in step beside words,
and with their three tenses in line,
the verbs climb the hill Golgotha.

The sky is above them
like a bird above a cemetery.
They stand upright
as though in front of a closed door
and a man lifts his arm and drives nails
into the past
into the present
into the future.

No one will ever come to bear witness.
The strokes of the hammer
become the rhythm of eternity.

Under the verbs stretches the hyperbole, earth,
and heaven, the metaphor, drifts above them.

1967, translated with
Wladimir Weidlé

THE JEWISH CEMETERY

The Jewish Cemetery near Leningrad:
a lame fence of rotten planks
and lying behind it side by side
lawyers, businessmen, musicians, revolutionaries.

They sang for themselves,
got rich for themselves,
died for others.
But always paid their taxes first;
        heeded the constabulary,
and in this inescapably material world
studied the Talmud,
        remained idealists.
Maybe they saw something more,
maybe believed blindly.
In any case they taught their children
        tolerance. But
        obstinacy. They
sowed no wheat,
        never sowed wheat,
simply lay down in the earth
        like grain
and fell asleep forever.
Earth was heaped over them,
candles were lit for them,
and on their day of the dead raw voices of famished
old men, the cold at their throats,
shrieked at them, "Eternal peace!"

Which they have found
        in the disintegration of matter,
remembering nothing
forgetting nothing

behind the lame fence of rotten planks
four kilometers past the streetcar terminal.

1967, translated with
Wladimir Weidlé

THE MONUMENT

Let us set up a monument
in the city, at the end of the long avenue,
or at the center of the big square,
a monument
that will stand out against any background
because it will be
quite well built and very realistic.
Let us set up a monument
that will not disturb anybody.

We will plant flowers
around the pedestal
and with the permission of the city fathers
we will lay out a little garden
where our children
will blink
at the great orange sun
and take the figure perched above them
for a well-known thinker
a composer
or a general.

I guarantee that flowers will appear
every morning
on the pedestal.
Let us set up a monument
that will not disturb anybody.
Even taxi drivers
will admire its majestic silhouette.
The garden will be a place
for rendezvous.
Let us set up a monument,
we will pass under it
        hurrying on our way to work,
foreigners will have their pictures taken
        standing under it,
we will splash it at night with the glare
        of floodlights.

Let us set up a monument to The Lie.

1967, translated with
Wladimir Weidlé

Selected Translations
1968–1978

This volume is for Richard Howard

~

CONTENTS 1968–1978

When Pope set out to translate Homer almost everything (as it appears to us) was known beforehand. He knew who most of his immediate readers would be: they had subscribed for the translations. They, in turn, knew—or thought they knew—who Homer was, and they knew the text, in the original. Both the subscribers and the translator took it for granted that the proper form for heroic verse, in English, must of course be the heroic couplet. Pope's work was expected to display the wit, elegance, and brilliance with which he could render a generally accepted notion of the Homeric poems into a familiar English verse form.

Since the eighteenth century, and especially since the beginning of modernism, more and more translations have been undertaken with the clear purpose of introducing readers (most of them, of course, unknown to the translators) to works they could not read in the original, by authors they might very well never have heard of, from cultures, traditions and forms with which they had no acquaintance. The contrast with Pope's situation is completed by the phenomenon that has appeared with growing frequency in the past half century, of poet-translators who do not, themselves, know the languages from which they are making their versions, but must rely, for their grasp of the originals, on the knowledge and work of others.

New—or different—assumptions mean different risks. New assumptions about the meaning of the word *translation*, whether or not they are defined, imply different aspects of the basic risk of all translation, however that is conceived. Which is no risk at all, in the terms of the most common cliché on the subject: that all translation is impossible. We seem to need it, just the same, insofar as we need literature at all. In our time, an individual or social literary culture without it is unthinkable. What is it that we think we need? We begin with the idea that it is the original—which means our relative conception of the original, as scholars, potential translators, or readers. At the outset, the notion is probably not consciously involved with any thought of the available means of translation. The "original" may even figure as something that might exist in more forms than one, just as it can be understood by more than one reader. But if we take a single word of any language and try to find an exact equivalent in another, even if the second language is closely akin to the first, we have to admit that it cannot be done. A single primary denotation may be shared; but the constellation of secondary meanings, the moving rings of associations, the etymological echoes, the sound and its own levels of association, do not have an equivalent because they cannot. If we put two words of a language together and repeat the attempt, the failure is still more obvious. Yet if we continue, we reach a point where some sequence of the first language conveys a dynamic unit, a rudiment of form. Some energy of the first language begins to be manifest, not only in single words but in the charge of their relationship. The surprising thing is that at this point the hope of translation does not fade altogether, but begins to emerge. Not that these rudiments of form in the original language can be matched—any more than individual words could be—with exact equivalents in another. But the imaginative force which they embody, and which single words embody in context, may suggest convocations of words in another language that will have a comparable thrust and sense.

By "rudiments of form" I mean recognizable elements of verbal order, not verse forms. I began with what I suppose was, and perhaps still is, a usual preconception about the latter: that fidelity in translating a poem should include an ambition to reproduce the original verse form. Besides, I started translating partly as a discipline, hoping that the process might help me to learn to write. Pound was one of the first to recommend the practice to me. He urged me to get as close to the original as possible, and told me to keep the rhyme scheme of the poems I was translating, too, if I could, for the exercise as much as anything else. He recommended that I look at the Spanish *romancero*, and I did; but it was almost fifteen years before I actually made versions of many of the *romances*—and without the original rhyme schemes. I kept to his advice, though, at the time. When I did come, gradually, to abandon more and more often the verse forms of poems that I was translating, I did not try to formulate any precise principle for doing so. Translation is a fairly empirical practice, usually, and the "reasons" for making particular choices, however well grounded in scholarship, are seldom wholly explicable. I would have recognized, probably quite early, a simple reluctance to sacrifice imagined felicities of the potential English version, to keep a verse pattern that was, in some sense, abstract. The preference seems to me practical, at least. I think I began to consider the subject more systematically when I was trying to decide on the best form for a translation of the *Chanson de Roland*. I had before me versions in blank verse both regular and more or less free, and one which contrived to keep not only the metrical structure of the Old French but the rhyme scheme: verse paragraphs known as *laisses*, sometimes many lines in length, each line ending with the same assonance. The result, in English, struck me as nothing more than an intellectual curiosity; unreadable. The word order of the lifeless English was contorted, line by line, to get those sounds to come out right. As for any of the virtues of the original that had moved hearers for centuries and contributed to the poem's survival over a thousand years, there was scarcely an indication of what they might have been. It's easy to multiply examples of this kind of translation. And yet it must be true that in translating, as in writing, formal verse, exigencies of the form itself occasionally contribute to the tension and resonance of the language. But I realized at some point that I had come to consider the verse conventions of original poems as part of the original language, in which they had a history of associations like that of individual words—something impossible to suggest in English simply by repeating the forms. Verse conventions are to a large degree matters of effects, which depend partly on a familiarity that cannot, of course, be translated at all. The effects of the convention in the new language can never be those it produces in the former one. This is true even with forms that have already been adopted. There would be certain obvious advantages in retaining the sonnet form in English, if translating a sonnet from Italian, but however successful the result, the sonnet form in English does not have the same associations it has in Italian; its effect is not the same; it does not mean the same thing. And sometimes an apparent similarity of form can be utterly misleading. The *Chanson de Roland*, again, for example. The original is in a ten-syllable line, and an English-speaking translator would naturally think, at first, of iambic pentameter. But if the poem is translated into any sort of blank verse in English (leaving aside the question of the relative vitality and brightness of that form in our age) the result is bound to evoke reverberations of the pentameter line in English from Marlowe through Tennyson—echoes that drown the real effect and value of the Old French verse.

I am describing a general tendency drawn from practice and not enunciating a principle. On the other side of the question, I am quite convinced of the impossibility of ever really translating the *Commedia* into any other language, yet I am grateful for several English versions of it, rhymed ones included, for insights into the original, and I recognize that certain of the rhymed translations—for short passages, at least—convey glimpses of what Dante was doing with his highly functional form. But I think that is a recommendation, also, for having many versions, by different hands, of a given poem. And if I had to choose one translation of Dante, it would be "literal," and in prose.

The whole practice is based on paradox: wanting the original leads us to want a translation. And the very notion of making or using a translation implies that it will not and cannot be the original. It must be something else. The original assumes the status of an impossible ideal, and our actual demands must concern themselves with the differences from it, with the manner of standing in stead of it. When I tried to formulate practically what I wanted of a translation, whether by someone else or by me, it was something like this: without deliberately altering the overt meaning of the original poem, I wanted the translation to represent, with as much life as possible, some aspect, some quality of the poem which made the translator think it was worth translating in the first place. I know I arrived at this apparently simple criterion by a process of elimination, remembering all the translations—whatever their other virtues—that I had read, or read at, and set down, thinking, "If the original is really *like* that, what could have been the point of translating it?"

The quality that is conveyed to represent the original is bound to differ with different translators, which is both a hazard and an opportunity. In the ideal sense in which one wants only the original, one wants the translator not to exist at all. In the practical sense in which the demand takes into account the nature of translation, the gifts—such as they are—of the translator are inescapably important. A poet-translator cannot write with any authority using someone else's way of hearing.

I have not set out to make translations that distorted the meaning of the originals on pretext of some other overriding originality. For several years I tried to maintain illogical barriers between what I translated and "my own" writing, and I think the insistence on the distinction was better than indulging in a view of everything being the (presumably inspired) same. But no single thing that anyone does is wholly separate from any other, and impulses, hopes, predilections toward writings as yet unconceived certainly must have manifested themselves in the choices of poems from other languages that I preferred to read and wanted to translate, and in the ways that I went about both. And whatever is done, translation included, obviously has some effect on what is written afterward. Except in a very few cases it would be hard for me to trace, in subsequent writings of my own, the influence of particular translations that I have made, but I know that the influences were and are there. The work of translation did teach, in the sense of forming, and making available, ways of hearing.

Re-examining and choosing the collection that was to be published as *Selected Translations 1948–1968* provided a natural occasion for reviewing what I thought I had been trying to do, and for considering what relation future translations of mine might conceivably bear to their originals. Since then I have tended, at least part of the time, toward a greater freedom from the original's verse conventions, with a view to suggesting some vitality of the original in forms native to English. The tendency was not altogether new, and has not been consistent. It was more like the recognition of a curiosity than a decision. In translating several modern poets from French and Spanish—Follain, Sabines—where the forms of the originals seemed to bear affinities with what is most hopeful in contemporary American poetry, I tried to suggest the original cadences as closely as I could. I had come to feel that one function of translation was to extend what could be said and heard in the new language—as original writing would do—but I was not anxious to conclude that there was only one way of doing so. I had been reading, for instance, Budge's translations of Egyptian Pyramid texts, and had been struck by how much more life—and to my way of hearing it, poetry—there was in the transliterations, hieroglyph by hieroglyph, than in the version Budge had edited into "good English." I wanted to leave some of the habits of English prose word order in abeyance, to see just how necessary they might or might not be, and find new tensions by other means—a process as old as poetic convention itself, a displacement of old forms with the elements of new ones. In the translations in *Asian Figures* I let the sequence of the ideograms (which in most cases I had in front of me, with their transliterations) suggest the English word order, where that could be done without destroying the sense. One object in working with sonnets of Quevedo's was to have the Spanish baroque phrasing evoke some of the same gnarled diction in English, and to echo the movement, the dramatic development of the sonnet form, but not the form itself. The translations from Ghalib, made from literal versions, scholarly material, and direct guidance supplied by Aijaz Ahmad, were part of the same impulse. My first drafts remained close to the original ghazal form, and both Aijaz and I thought them papery. As he planned to include in the eventual publication the original texts, literal versions, and his notes on vocabulary, the whole point of the enterprise was to produce something else from the material—poems in English, if possible. The rule was that they were not to conflict with Ghalib's meaning, phrase by phrase, but that they need not render everything, either. Translation was viewed as fragmentary in any case; one could choose the fragments, to some degree. Considering the inadequacy of any approach to translation, I had been thinking of Cézanne's painting the Montagne St. Victoire over and over, each painting new, each one another mountain, each one different from the one he had started to paint. I imagined that in translating a poem something might be gained by making a series of versions bringing out different possibilities. I still think so, though I realize that versions, however many, from a single poet-translator are likely to sound like variants of each other, and echo the translator's ear at least as clearly as they do the original.

The Ghalib translations are among those made without any firsthand knowledge of the original language, as I have explained. I don't know that such a procedure can either be justified or condemned altogether, any more than translation as a whole can be. Auden, for one, thought it the best possible way of going about it. I suspect it depends on the circumstances—who is doing the work, and their relation to each other and to the poetry they are translating. I have had my doubts about working this way, and have resolved several times not to do any more translation of this kind, but I have succumbed repeatedly to particular material.

I should make it clear that the only languages from which I can translate directly are Romance languages, and that I am less familiar with Italian and Portuguese than with French and Spanish. All the translations from other sources, in this collection, were based on someone else's knowledge.

W.S.M.

A NOTE ON THE LANGUAGES

QUECHUA is a major language of the Andean plateaus. At one time it was a principal language of the Incan Empire.

TZOTZIL and TZELTAL are Mayan languages of the highlands of Chiapas in southern Mexico. Zinacantan and Tenejapa are villages; TZOTZIL is spoken in the former, TZELTAL in the latter.

MALGACHE (or MALAGASY, as it is anglicized) is the language of Madagascar.

Julianus, Prefect of Egypt | Greek
5th century A.D.

Though you rule the dead, under the earth, who never smile,
    Persephone, welcome the shade of the gentle laughter,
Democritus. It was laughter alone that led
    your mother away from grief, when her heart was sore,
        after she lost you.

1971

Automedon | Greek

EPITAPH FOR CLEONICUS

You who will die, watch over your life; don't set sail
        at the wrong season, for at best no man lives long.
Poor Cleonicus, so impatient to reach
        bright Thasos, trading out of hollow Syria,
trading, Cleonicus, sailing just as the Pleiades
        were setting, so that you and the Pleiades sank together.

1971

Antiphilos | Greek
1st century A.D.

GIFTS TO A LADY

I've not much of my own, lady, mistress, but I
      believe that the man who's yours heart and soul stands
a full head above most men's riches.
      Accept this tunic, the soft pile of flowered purple,
this rose-red wool, this nard in a green glass
      for your dark hair. I want the first to enfold your body,
the wool to draw out the skill of your fingers,
      the scent to find its way through your hair.

1971

A QUINCE PRESERVED THROUGH THE WINTER, GIVEN TO A LADY

I'm a quince, saved over from last year, still fresh,
      my skin young, not spotted or wrinkled, downy as the newborn,
as though I were still among my leaves. Seldom
      does winter yield such gifts, but for you, my queen,
even the snows and frosts bear harvests like this.

1971

ON THE DEATH OF THE FERRYMAN, GLAUCUS

Glaucus, pilot of the Nessus Strait, born
      on the coast of Thasos, skilled sea-plowman,
who moved the tiller unerringly even in his sleep,
      old beyond reckoning, a rag of a sailor's life,
even when death came would not leave his weathered deck.
      They set fire to the husk with him under it
so the old man might sail his own boat to Hades.

1971

Michelangelo | Italian 1475-1564

Very dear though it was I have bought you
a little whatever-it-is for its sweet smell
since by the scent often I find the way
Wherever you are wherever I am
beyond all doubt I will be clear and certain
If you hide yourself from me I pardon you
Taking it always with you where you go
even if I were quite blind I would find you

1973

Giacomo Leopardi | Italian
1798-1837

THE INFINITE

I always loved this hill by itself
and this line of bushes that hides
so much of the farthest horizon from sight.
But sitting looking out I imagine spaces
beyond this one, each without end,
and silences more than human, and a stillness
under it all, until my heart is drawn
to the edge of fear. And when the wind
rustles through the undergrowth near me
endlessly I compare its voice
with the infinite silence. I remember eternity
and the ages dead, and the present,
alive, and the sound of it. So in this
immensity my thinking drowns,
and sinking is sweet to me in this sea.

1971

João Cabral de Melo Neto

Portuguese
1920-1999

THE MAN FROM UP-COUNTRY TALKING

The man from up-country coats his talk:
the words come out of him like wrapped candy
(candy words, pills) in the icing
of a smooth intonation, sweetened.
While under the talk the core of stone
keeps hardening, the stone almond
from the rocky tree back where he comes from:
it can express itself only in stone.

That's why the man from up-country says little:
the stone words ulcerate the mouth
and it hurts to speak in the stone language;
those to whom it's native speak by main force.
Furthermore, that's why he speaks slowly:
he has to take up the words carefully,
he has to sweeten them with his tongue, candy them;
well, all this work takes time.

1969

TWO OF THE FESTIVALS OF DEATH

Solemn receptions given by death:
death, dressed for an unveiling;
and ambiguously: dressed like an orator
and like the statue that's to be unveiled.
In the coffin, half coffin half pedestal,
death unveils himself more than he dies;
and in duplicate: now he's his own statue,
now he's himself, alive, for the occasion.

Children's picnics given by death:
children's funerals in the northeast:
no one over thirteen admitted,
no adults allowed, even walking behind.
Party half outing half picnic,
in the open air, nice for a day when school's out;
the children who go play dolls
or else that's what they really are.

1969

THE DRAFTED VULTURE

I

When the droughts hit the backlands, they make
the vulture into a civil servant—free no more.
He doesn't try to escape. He's known for a long time
that they'd put his technique and his touch to use.
He says nothing of services rendered, of diplomas
that entitle him to better pay.
He serves the drought-dealers like an altar boy,
with a greenhorn zeal, veteran though he is,
mercifully dispatching some who may not be dead,
when in private life he cares only for bona fide corpses.

II

Though the vulture's a conscript, you can soon tell
from his demeanor that he's a real professional:
his self-conscious air, hunched and advisory,
his umbrella completeness, the clerical smoothness
with which he acts, even in a minor capacity—
an unquestioning liberal professional.

1969

INSTRUCTS HOW ALL THINGS FORETELL DEATH

for Inés Kinnell

My country I saw its walls
that were strong at one time
but are going
weary of age his round

I went out to fields saw the sun
drinking streams
only thawed
and from the mount the crying herds
whose shadows stole
from the day its light

I went into my house
defaced
ruined old dwelling place
my staff more bent
also weaker

age had beat down my sword
and there was nowhere
to turn my eyes toward
but death also was coming there

1968

LOVE CONSTANT BEYOND DEATH

Last of the shadows may close my eyes
goodbye then white day
and with that my soul untie
its dear wishing

yet will not forsake
memory of this shore where it burned
but still burning swim
that cold water again
careless of the stern law

soul that kept God in prison
veins that to love led such fire
marrow that flamed in glory

not their heeding will leave
with their body
but being ash will feel
dust be dust in love

1968

Pedro Salinas

Spanish
1892–1951

This iron chain,
heavy as it is, seems
light to me, I don't feel it.
There's another chain made
of waves, lands, winds,
smiles, sighs,
that binds me I don't know where,
that enslaves me to that master
I don't know, that master…

1968

I can't see you but I know
you're right there on the other side
of a thin wall
of bricks and lime where
you'd hear if I called.
But I won't call.
I'll call you tomorrow
when not seeing you
makes me think you're still
there close beside me
and that all I need today
is the voice I withheld
yesterday.
Tomorrow when you're
there on the other side
of a thin wall of winds
skies, years.

1968

HER ABSENCE

You're not here. What I see of you,
a body, is a shadow, a trick.
Your soul has gone where you
yourself will be tomorrow.
Still this afternoon offers me
false hostages, aimless
smiles, idle gestures,
a love distracted.
You wanted to go and it took you
where you wanted to be,
far from here, where you
are saying to me,
"Here I am, with you, look."
And you point to your absence.

1968

GOODBYE

We're leaning
on the railing
over the water of goodbye.
It's neither muddy nor empty.
It has clouds, leaves in it, flights
in it
coming and going, and going
without a sound.

Numbers are floating there, letters,
loose, on top of it;
they don't add up to anything, don't
say anything.
Elysian figures, letters

in the garb of paradise,
assumption and holiday,
ready for another life.
You're much clearer in the water goodbye
than in your face.
You're much clearer in the water goodbye
than in my soul.
Now you'll never leave
here.
You'll live that way, outside
your face and my soul,
a third, made of you and me,
new,
cool daughter of goodbye.
Live:
see ourselves in goodbye.

1968

FURTHER QUESTION

Why do I ask where you are
if I'm not blind
and you're not absent?

If I see you
go and come,
you, your tall body
ending in a voice
as a flame ends in smoke
in the air, untouchable.

And I ask you, yes,
and I ask you
what you're made of

and whose you are
and you open your arms
and show me
the tall image of yourself
and say it's mine.

And I go on asking, forever.

1968

Not in marble palaces,
not in months, no, nor in numbers,
never treading the ground:
in frail worlds without weight
we have lived together.
Time was scarcely
reckoned in minutes:
one minute was a century,
a life, a love.
Roofs sheltered us.
Less than roofs, clouds.
Less than clouds: skies.
Still less: air, nothing.
Crossing
seas made of twenty tears,
ten of yours ten of mine,
we came to beads
of gold,
immaculate islands, deserted,
without flowers or flesh:
so small a lodging,
and of glass, for a love
able to reach, by itself,
the greatest longing,
and that asked no help

of ships or time.
Opening
enormous galleries
in the grains of sand,
we discovered the mines
of flames or of chance.
And all
hanging from that thread
that was held—by whom?
That's why our life doesn't seem
to have been lived.
Elusive as quicksilver,
it left neither wake
nor track. If you want
to remember it, don't look
in footsteps or memory,
where people always look.
Don't look in the soul,
in the shadows, in the lips.
Look carefully in the palm
of the hand: empty.

1968

Vicente Huidobro | Spanish
1893–1948

POETRY IS A HEAVENLY CRIME

I am absent but deep in this absence
There is the waiting for myself
And this waiting is another form of presence
The waiting for my return
I am in other objects
I am away travelling giving a little of my life
To some trees and some stones
That have been waiting for me many years

They got tired of waiting for me and sat down

I'm not here and I'm here
I'm absent and I'm present in a state of waiting
They wanted my language so they could express themselves
And I wanted theirs to express them
This is the ambiguity, the horrible ambiguity

Tormented wretched
I'm moving inward on these soles
I'm leaving my clothes behind
My flesh is falling away on all sides
And my skeleton's putting on bark

I'm turning into a tree How often I've turned into other things…
It's painful and full of tenderness

I could cry out but it would scare off the transubstantiation
Must keep silence Wait in silence

1970

MY WHOLE LIFE

Here once again the memorable lips, unique and like yours.
I am this groping intensity that is a soul.
I have got near to happiness and have stood in the shadow of suffering.
I have crossed the sea.
I have known many lands; I have seen one woman and two or three men.
I have loved a girl who was fair and proud, with a Spanish quietness.
I have seen the city's edge, an endless sprawl where the sun goes down
      tirelessly, over and over.
I have relished many words.
I believe deeply that this is all and that I will neither see nor accomplish
      new things.
I believe that my days and my nights, in their poverty and their riches,
      are the equal of God's and of all men's.

1968

TO A MINOR POET OF THE GREEK ANTHOLOGY

Where now is the memory
of the days that were yours on earth, and wove
joy with sorrow, and made a universe that was your own?

The river of years has lost them
from its numbered current; you are a word in an index.

To others the gods gave glory that has no end:
inscriptions, names on coins, monuments, conscientious historians;
all that we know of you, eclipsed friend,
is that you heard the nightingale one evening.

Among the asphodels of the Shadow, your shade, in its vanity,
must consider the gods ungenerous.

But the days are a web of small troubles
and is there a greater blessing
than to be the ash of which oblivion is made?

Above other heads the gods kindled
the inexorable light of glory, which peers into the secret parts and
        discovers each separate fault;
glory, that at last shrivels the rose it reveres;
they were more considerate with you, brother.

In the rapt evening that will never be night
you listen without end to Theocritus's nightingale.

1968

THE POET TELLS OF HIS FAME

The rim of the sky is the measure of my glory,
The libraries of the East argue over my verses,
The rulers seek me out to fill my mouth with gold,
The angels already know my last couplet by heart.
The tools of my art are humiliation and anguish.
Oh if only I had been born dead!

from the Divan of Abulcasim
El Hadrami (12th century)

1968

Nicanor Parra | Spanish born 1914

A MAN

A man's mother is very sick
He goes out to find a doctor
He's crying
In the street he sees his wife in the company of another man
They're holding hands
He follows them a short distance
From tree to tree
He's crying
Now he meets a friend from his youth
It's years since we've seen each other!
They go on to a bar
They talk, laugh
The man goes out to the patio for a piss
He sees a young girl
It's night
She's washing dishes
The man goes over to her
He takes her by the waist
They waltz
They go out into the street together
They laugh
There's an accident
The girl's lost consciousness
The man goes to telephone
He's crying
He comes to a house with lights on
He asks for a telephone
Somebody knows him
Hey stay and have something to eat

No
Where's the telephone
Have something to eat, hey eat something
Then go
He sits down to eat
He drinks like a condemned man
He laughs
They get him to recite something
He recites it
He ends up sleeping under a desk

1970

SONG OF THE FOREIGNER

Travelling man
come into this room
coming out of bathroom
sit on precious chair
in front of birror
oped his fly

The cloud cover the sun
I cover the cloud with left hand
I spit blood
So bad danger the sky send

My going in cemetery
me cry very much for dead one used to married to
me put urn in nitz
not let nobody touch him
I kiss him urn—I hug him urn—I everything

I buy him more prettiest urn
with precious crucifix
I put him myself in coffin
I cry—I laugh because with great suffering
I customer and sell you little comb cheap

1970

PROPOSALS

I'm sad I've got nothing to eat
nobody cares about me
there shouldn't be any beggars
I've been saying the same thing for years

I propose that instead of butterflies
lobsters should move in the gardens
—I think that would be a lot better—
can you imagine a world without beggars?

I propose that we all turn catholic
or communist or whatever you like
it's only a difference of words
I propose that we purify the water

with the authority given me by my beggar's stick
I propose that the pope grow a moustache

I'm starting to feel faint with hunger
I propose that they give me a sandwich
and to end the monotony I propose
that the sun should rise in the west

1970

I Jehovah decree

that they get it over with once and for all
I'm giving the solar system the slip

everything back into the womb
I'm saying it's over finished and done with

nobody's escaping
everything over with in one stroke
why beat around the bush

great thing the Vietnam War
great thing the Prostate Operation
I Jehovah decree old age

you people make me laugh
you people give me the creeps
only a born moron
could get down on his knees and worship a statue

frankly I don't know what to tell you
we're on the brink of the Third World War
and nobody seems to have noticed

if you destroy the world
do you think I'm going to create it over again?

1970

EVERYTHING USED TO LOOK GOOD TO ME

Now everything looks bad to me

an old telephone with a little bell
was enough to make me the happiest creature alive
an armchair — almost anything

Sunday mornings
I'd go to the flea market
and come back with a wall clock
— anyway with the case —
or with a pensioned-off victrola
to my shack at La Reina
where Chamaco was waiting for me
and the lady who used to be his mother
in those days

those were happy days
or at least nights without pain

1970

Juan José Arreola | Spanish
1918–2001

ELEGY

Those vague scars that can be seen there among the plowed fields are the ruins of the camp of Nobilior. Farther on rise the military positions of Castillejo, Renieblas, and Peña Redona...

Nothing is left of the distant city except one hill heavy with silence. And next to it, running beside it, that ruin of a river. The little stream Merdancho hums its ballad refrain, and resounds with epic greatness only in the sudden flash floods of June.

This tranquil plain witnessed the succession of incompetent generals. Nobilior, Lepidus, Furius Filus, Caius Hostilius Mancinus... And among them the poet Lucilius, who sauntered there with the airs of a conqueror, and returned to Rome ill-used and beaten, his sword and his lyre both dragging, and his sharp tongue blunted.

Legions upon legions were shattered against those invincible walls. Thousands of soldiers went down under the arrows, despair, the winter. Until one day the enraged Scipio loomed up on the horizon like an avenging wave and seized in his unyielding hands the tough neck of Numancia, month after month without letting go.

1969

THE CAVE

Nothing but horror, pure and empty. That is the cave of Tribenciano. A stone void in the bowels of the earth. A cavity, long and rounded like an egg. Two hundred meters long, eighty wide. A dome in every direction, of marbled smooth stone.

There are seventy steps going down to the cave, arranged in flights of different lengths, along a natural fissure that opens like an ordinary crack in the ground. What does one go down to? At one time it was to die.

There are bones on the cave floor, and quantities of bone dust. No one knows whether the nameless victims went down of their own free will or were sent there by some special order. And whose?

Some students of the cave are convinced that it is not the abode of any cruel mystery. They say that it all has to do with an ancient cemetery, perhaps Etruscan, perhaps Ligurian. But no one can remain in that cavern for more than five minutes: he runs the risk of completely losing his mind.

Men of science prefer to explain the fainting that overcomes those who venture inside by saying that underground gas seeps into the cave. But no one knows what kind of gas it might be or where it comes from. It may be that what seizes a man there is the horror of pure space: nothing, in its concave muteness.

No more is known about the cave of Tribenciano. Thousands of cubic meters of nothing in its round pot. Nothing, in a rind of stone. Holding death dust.

1969

TELEMACHUS

Wherever there's a fight I'll be on the side that falls. Now it's heroes or thugs.

I'm tied by the neck to the slave concept carved on the oldest standing stones. I'm the dying warrior under Asurbanipal's chariot, and the calcined bone in the ovens of Dachau.

Hector and Menelaus, France and Germany, and the two drunks who push in each other's faces in the bar wear me out with their disputes. Wherever I turn my eyes the landscape of the world is hidden by an enormous Veronica's Veil showing the face of the Despised Good.

I the observer of force see which of the combatants starts the fight, and I want to be on no one's side. Because I also am two: the one who strikes and the one who receives the blows.

Man against man. Any bets?

Ladies and gentlemen, there is no salvation. The game is being lost within ourselves. At this moment the Devil's playing with the white pieces.

1969

DEER

Outside space and time the deer wander, at once swift and languid, and no one knows whether their true place is in immobility or in movement; they combine the two in such a way that we are forced to place them in eternity.

Inert or dynamic, they keep changing the natural horizon, and they perfect our ideas of time, space, and the laws of moving bodies. Made expressly to solve the ancient paradox, they are at once Achilles and the tortoise, the bow and the arrow. They run without ever overtaking. They stop and something remains always outside them, galloping.

The deer cannot stand still, but moves forward like an apparition, whether it be among real trees or out of a grove in a legend: Saint Hubert's stag bearing a cross between his antlers, or the doe that gives suck to Genevieve de Brabant. Wherever they are encountered, the male and the female compose the same fabulous pair.

Quarry without peer, all of us mean to take it, even if only with the eyes. And if Juan de Yepes tells us that what he pursued, when hunting, was so high, so high—he is not referring to the earthly dove, but to the deer: profound, unattainable, and in flight.

1969

Roberto Juarroz

Spanish
1925-1995

Sometimes my hands wake me up.
They're making or taking apart something without me
while I'm asleep,
something terribly human,
concrete like the back or pocket of a man.

I hear them from inside my sleep,
working out there,
but when I open my eyes they're still.
Just the same
I've thought that maybe I'm a man
because of what they do
with their gestures and not mine,
with their God and not mine,
with their death, if they die too.

I don't know how to make a man.
Maybe my hands make one while I'm asleep
and when it's finished
they wake me up altogether
and show it to me.

1971

A man spells out his tiredness.
All at once as he spells
he meets some strange capital letters,
unexpectedly alone,
unexpectedly tall.
They weigh more on the tongue.
They weigh more but they get away

faster and hardly
can they be spoken.
His heart crowds into the roads
where death is exploding.
And he meets, as he goes on spelling,
bigger and bigger capital letters.
And a great fear chokes him
of finding a word
written all in capitals
and not being able to pronounce it.

1971

There will come a day
when we won't need to push on the panes for them to fall,
nor hammer the nails for them to hold,
nor walk on the stones to keep them quiet,
nor drink the faces of women for them to smile.

It will be the beginning of the great union.
Even God will learn how to talk,
and the air and the light
will enter their cave of shy eternities.

Then there'll be no more difference between your eyes and
        your belly,
nor between my words and my mouth.
The stones will be like your breasts
and I will make my verses with my hands
so that nobody can be mistaken.

1971

Life draws a tree
and death draws another one.
Life draws a nest
and death copies it.
Life draws a bird
to live in the nest
and right away death
draws another bird.

A hand that draws nothing
wanders among the drawings
and at times moves one of them.
For example:
a bird of life
occupies death's nest
on the tree that life drew.

Other times
the hand that draws nothing
blots out one drawing of the series.
For example:
the tree of death,
holds the nest of death,
but there's no bird in it.

And other times
the hand that draws nothing
itself changes
into an extra image
in the shape of a bird,
in the shape of a tree,
in the shape of a nest.
And then, only then,
nothing's missing and nothing's left over.
For example:
two birds

occupy life's nest
in death's tree.

Or life's tree
holds two nests
with only one bird in them.

Or a single bird
lives in the one nest
on the tree of life
and the tree of death.

1970

I'm awake.
I'm asleep.
I'm dreaming that I'm awake.
I'm dreaming that I'm asleep.
I'm dreaming that I'm dreaming.

I'm dreaming that I'm dreaming
that I'm awake.
I'm dreaming that I'm dreaming
that I'm asleep.
I'm dreaming that I'm dreaming
that I'm dreaming.

I'm awake.

1971

If we knew the point
where something is going to break,
where the thread of kisses will be cut,
where a look will no longer meet another,
where the heart will leap toward another place,
we could put another point on that point
or at least go with it to its breaking.

If we knew the point
where something is going to melt into something,
where the desert will meet the rain,
where the embrace will touch life itself,
where my death will come closer to yours,
we could unwind that point like a streamer,
or at least sing it till we died.

If we knew the point
where something will always be something,
where the bone will not forget the flesh,
where the fountain is mother to another fountain,
where the past will never be past,
we could retain that point and erase all the others,
or at least keep it in a safer place.

   (*to Laura*)

                                        1971

Jaime Sabines | Spanish
1926–1999

FROM *DIARIO SEMANARIO*

At midnight, at the last moment of August, I think sadly about the leaves that keep falling from the calendars. I feel that I am the tree of the calendars.

Every day, my child, that goes away forever, leaves me asking: if someone who loses a parent is an orphan, if someone who has lost a wife is a widower, what is the word for someone who loses a child? What is the word for someone who loses time? And if I myself am time, what is the word for me if I lose myself?

Day and night, not Monday or Tuesday, nor August or September, day and night are the only measure of our duration. To exist is to last,—to open your eyes and close them.

Every night at this time, forever, I am the one who has lost the day. (Even though I may feel, in the heart of this time, the dawn climbing, like the fruit in the branches of the peach tree.)

1971

I HAVE EYES TO SEE

I have eyes to see in this night
something of what I am, my hearing is hearing.
I am in this room, so are my dreams.

Back of each shadow there's something of mine.
There's one sitting on each chair, dark,
and at my feet, in bed, they're seeing me.
I believe they're like me, they bear my name
and they emerge from things, like mirrors.

It's already a long time
since we last assembled.
Now I give them lodging
humbly,
I give them my body.

I come together again at night, I open my eyes,
I wet them with this darkness full of dream.
Only my heart on top of the sheet
still beating.

1971

FROM THE BODIES

From the blue and black bodies
that walk at times through my soul
come voices and signs that someone interprets.
It's dark as the sun
this desire. Mysterious and grave
as an ant dragging away the wing of a butterfly
or as the yes that we say when things ask us
—do you want to live?

1971

I'M OUT TO FIND A MAN

I'm out to find a man who looks like me
to give him my name and my wife and my son,
my books and my debts.
I'm going looking for someone to give him my soul,
my fate, my death.

With what pleasure I'd do it,
with what tenderness I'd leave myself in his hands!

1971

YOU HAVE WHAT I LOOK FOR

You have what I look for, what I long for, what I love,
you have it.
The fist of my heart is beating, calling.
I thank the stories for you,
I thank your mother and your father
and death who has not seen you.
I thank the air for you.
You are elegant as wheat,
delicate as the outline of your body.
I have never loved a slender woman
but you have made my hands fall in love,
you moored my desire,
you caught my eyes like two fish.
And for this I am at your door, waiting.

1975

Roque Dalton

Spanish
1935-1975

THE CONCEITED

I'd be wonderful at being dead.

Then my vices would shine like ancient jewels
with those delicious colors of poison.

There'd be flowers of every scent on my tomb
and the adolescents would imitate my expressions of joy,
my occult words of anguish.

Maybe somebody'd say I was loyal and good.
But you'd be the only one who'd remember
the way I looked into eyes.

1971

Anonymous | Russian
19th century

PILGRIM SONGS

I

Come children of the same family
listen to the word
         of the Lord
what it says about our life

the life of someone on earth
         is like the grass growing in the fields
the mind in each person
         blossoms like the flowers

and to the last evening
         a body is happy
but in the morning
         it lies in its grave
the quick legs
         out from under it
the white hands fallen

there was not even time
to press the hands
to the racing heart

oh you there what good is it
for them to wash your dead body
when you never bathed it in tears
         before the Lord

oh you there what good is it
wrapping you in vestments

when you never wrapped yourself
      in vestments of the spirit

oh you there what good is it
lighting candles over you
when you kept no lamp burning
      in your heart
      before the Lord

oh you there what good is it
performing a service over you
when you never performed
      what God commanded

oh you there what good is it
to go with your corpse
      to God's church
when you had no spiritual father
      and never repented your sins

all your glory has gone now
all you possessed stayed here

the soul has said goodbye
      to its white body
and the mind is parting from its head
      from that precious one

and for all times
have mercy on us

II

Our life on earth
      is like the grass growing
and the mind in us
      is like the opened flowers

in the evening
      a body is happy
by morning that same one
      lies in the grave
bright eyes clouded
      quick legs gone from under

if you want to escape
      eternal pain
take a candle of pure gold
      and its adornments
enter into joy
      with the bridegroom
and reign forever

oh you there go up
onto the mountain of Zion
and listen a while
          oh you
to the loud trumpet sound
the trumpet sounding the truth
the herald of heaven

1977, translated with Alla Burago

Alexander Blok | Russian
1880-1921

Beyond the mountains beyond the forests
beyond the dust of the roads
beyond the grave mounds
under other skies you flower

Whiteness will spread on the mountain
but spring will come back to the valley
and I will recall with an older sadness
my past as though it were yesterday

In the grief of my dreams I will know you
and I will seize in my palms
your gentle hand that has borne miracles
and repeat the distance in your name

September 30, 1915

1968, translated with
Olga Carlisle

Osip Mandelstam

Russian
1891–1938

LENINGRAD

I've come back to my city. These are my own old tears,
my own little veins, the swollen glands of my childhood.

So you're back. Open wide. Swallow
the fish oil from the river lamps of Leningrad.

Open your eyes. Do you know this December day,
the egg yolk with the deadly tar beaten into it?

Petersburg! I don't want to die yet!
You know my telephone numbers.

Petersburg! I've still got the addresses:
I can look up dead voices.

I live on back stairs, and the bell,
torn-out nerves and all, jangles in my temples.

And I wait till morning for guests that I love,
and rattle the door in its chains.

Leningrad. December 1930

1972, translated with
Clarence Brown

Your thin shoulders are for turning red under whips,
turning red under whips, and flaming in the raw cold.

Your child's fingers are for lifting flatirons,
for lifting flatirons, and for knotting cords.

Your tender soles are for walking on broken glass,
walking on broken glass, across bloody sand.

And I'm for burning like a black candle lit for you,
for burning like a black candle that dare not pray.

1934

1972, translated with
Clarence Brown

Now I'm dead in the grave with my lips moving
and every schoolboy repeating the words by heart.

The earth is rounder in Red Square than anywhere,
all one side of a hardened will.

The earth in Red Square is rounder than anywhere.
No one would think it was so light of heart

bending back all the way down to the rice growing
on the last day of the last slave on the globe.

Voronezh. May 1935

1972, translated with
Clarence Brown

How dark it gets along the Kama.
The cities kneel by the river on oaken knees.

Draped in cobwebs, beard with beard,
black firs and their reflections run back into their childhood.

The water leaned into fifty-two pairs of oars,
pushed them upstream, downstream, to Kazan and Cherdyn.*

There I floated with a curtain across the window,
a curtain across the window, and the flame inside was my head.

And my wife was with me there five nights without sleeping,
five nights awake keeping an eye on the guards.

    Voronezh. May 1935

                              1972, translated with
                              Clarence Brown

Today is all beak and no feathers
and it's staying that way. Why?
And a gate by the sea gazes at me
out of anchors and fogs.

Quietly, quietly warships are gliding
through faded water,
and in canals gaunt as pencils
under the ice the leads go on blackening.

    Voronezh. December 9–28, 1936

                              1972, translated with
                              Clarence Brown

---

*After his first arrest, Mandelstam was exiled to the town of Cherdyn in the Urals.
With his wife by his side he made part of the jouney there along the river Kama.

Mounds of human heads are wandering into the distance.
I dwindle among them. Nobody sees me. But in books
much loved, and in children's games I shall rise
from the dead to say the sun is shining.

1936–1937?

1972, translated with
Clarence Brown

THE LAST SUPPER

The heaven of the supper fell in love with the wall.
It filled it with cracks. It fills them with light.
It fell into the wall. It shines out there
in the form of thirteen heads.

And that's my night sky, before me,
and I'm the child standing under it,
my back getting cold, an ache in my eyes,
and the wall-battering heaven battering me.

At every blow of the battering ram
stars without eyes rain down,
new wounds in the last supper,
the unfinished mist on the wall.

Voronezh. March 9, 1937

1972, translated with
Clarence Brown

Lars Norén | Swedish born 1944

Today everything
is earnest and hushed.
As at the death of a queen
when the radio changes from light music
to Mozart or Bach.
I don't know why.
Since she isn't listening.
I can almost see
how people leave
each other, how silence
works in the fading fabrics
and how the solitary
gray wasp gropes its way
into its death sleep
in the wound of the dry mountain tree.

1975, translated with
Gunnar Harding

Maybe this road
leads nowhere but someone
is coming from there

1976, translated with
Gunnar Harding

ON NELLY SACHS

Toward the end
her eyes grew
younger and younger
as though they had been watching
what can be understood but not said
They weighed almost nothing
and must have been like the rabbit's
breath in winter air after it has been shot

1976, translated with
Gunnar Harding

When I travel back to my
own birth and existence
there is no mother there
and I have to give birth to her

1976, translated with
Gunnar Harding

Whatever place
I come on trouble
my death will not be there

I shall pass through

though there may be many arrows
I shall reach
where I am going

as the heart of a man should be
mine is

1969

If all of me is still there
    when spring comes
    I'll make a hundred poles

    and put something on top
    sun

    for you
    you

right there I'll make a small sweat lodge
    it's cold
    I'll sprinkle charcoal

    at the end of it
    my death

sun
    it will all be for you

I want to be still there
    that's why I'll do it

    thank you

I want to be alive

If my people multiply
    I'll make it for you

I'm saying
    may no one be sick

    so I make it

    so

                1970

If there is someone above
who knows what happens

You

today I have trouble
give me something to make it
not so

if there is someone inside the earth
who knows what happens

I have trouble today
give me something
to make it not so

whatever makes these things
now just as I am
I have enough

give me just for me
my death

I have enough sadness

1969

Your way
        is turning bad

        and nobody but you
        is there

1970

Child listen
        I am singing

        with my ear on the ground

        and we love you

1970

I am climbing
     everywhere is

coming up

1970

I am making
     a wind come here

it's coming

1970

Heaven
Earth
     always there

the old fill up
     with trouble

don't be afraid

1970

Anonymous | Quechua
Incan
adapted from Spanish

PRAYER

Oh you

from whom it came
        comes

        you
lord of what is

whether you're
        a man
whether you're
        a woman
        lord
of what's born

whatever you are
lord of the sight beyond

where are you

you above at this moment
you below at this moment

presence
throne scepter
        shining around them

hear
me

maybe the sky is your floor
maybe the sea is your roof
          maker of above and below

as we are you made us
lord above lords

my eyes are weak
with longing to see you
          only with longing
to know you

make it be
          that I see you
make it be
          that I know you
make it be
          that I hold you in my thought
make it be
          that you are clear in my mind

look at me
for you know me

sun and moon
day and night
spring and winter
you set them in order
          you

          from whom it came
          comes
all of them run
          the course you marked out for them
all of them reach
          the goal you set for them
wherever you wanted it

you bearing
the king's scepter

hear me
choose me

do not let me grow tired
do not let me die

1970

PRAYER

Come closer truth from above us
truth from below us

who made the form of the world

    you
    who let it all exist

    who alone made humans

ten times with eyes full of darkness
    I must worship you

    saying Brightness

    stretched out before you

look at me
    lord
    notice me

and your rivers your waterfalls
your birds
give me your
life
all you can

help me to call
with your voices

even now we taste
　　the joy of your will
　　and we remember it all
　　we are happy

even so we are filled
　　as we go away
　　as we go

　　　　　　　　　　　　1970

Where are you where are you going
they say
and we still have to go on

sun and moon go past
　　and go past
　　six months to get from Cuzco to Quito

at the foot of Tayo we'll rest

fear nothing
lord Inca fear nothing
we're going with you we'll get there together

　　　　　　　　　　　　1970

I'm bringing up a fly
        with golden wings
        bringing up a fly
        with eyes burning

it carries death
        in its eyes of fire
carries death
        in its golden hair
        in its gorgeous wings

in a green bottle
        I'm bringing it up

        nobody knows
        if it drinks

        nobody knows
        if it eats

at night it goes wandering
        like a star

        wounding to death
        with red rays
        from its eyes of fire

it carries love
        in its eyes of fire
        flashes in the night
        its blood
        the love it bears in its breast

insect of night
fly bearing death

in a green bottle
I'm bringing it up
        I love it
        that much

but nobody
        no
nobody knows

if I give it to drink
nobody knows if I feed it

                                1970

When you find you're alone on the island in the river
your father won't be there
to call you
        aloo
        my daughter
your mother won't be able
to reach you
        aloo
        my daughter

only the royal duck will stay near you
with the rain in its eyes
with tears of blood
        with the rain in its eyes
        tears of blood

and even the royal duck will leave you
when the waves of the river
        boil
when the waves
        race on the river

but then I'll go and stay near you
singing
       I'll steal her young heart
       on the island

       her young heart
       in the storm

                      1970

It's today I'm supposed
       to go away
I won't
       I'll go
       tomorrow

you'll see me go
       playing a flute
made from a bone of a fly

       carrying a flag
made from a spider's web

       beating an ant's egg
drum

with a hummingbird's nest for a hat
       with my head
       in a hummingbird's nest

                      1970

Anonymous | Tzeltal
Tenejapa

PRAYER TO THE CORN IN THE FIELD

Sacred food
sacred bones

don't go to another house
don't go at all

come straight in to us
stay right on the trail

to the house
to your bed

don't go crying like an orphan
to another plant

another stone
another cave

kernels that fall out of you
that I didn't find to pick up

if there are those of you
who were taken from your places

by the mountain lion
by the squirrel

by the coyote
by the fox

by the pig
by the thief

come back along the trail
to our house

the whole time
to our place

don't get smaller
going away

from our feet
from our hands

1971, from a literal version
by Katherine B. Branstetter's
informant Am Perez Mesa

STORY OF THE LAZY MAN AND THE ANTS

A man was very lazy at working.
A man feels he will never be finished working.
A man slept at his work.
A man didn't work much every day.
A man felt like working only a little bit every day.
Every day a man sleeps at his work.
When his work grabs him he scratches his head a lot.
Every day a man is just yawning at his work.
There is the sun.
Went to see the lazy man.
When the sun gets to the lazy man
He finds him sleeping at his work.
The lazy man is crying through his nose in his sleep. He is snoring.
The sun says, "What a lazy man at his work! What a lot he sleeps!"
The sun grabbed dust in his hand.
Three times.

The sun threw three handfuls of dust
Where the lazy man was sleeping.
The sun made the dust turn into ants.
Then the dust turned into ants.
The ants of earth fell onto the lazy man
Where he was sleeping.
The lazy man opened his eyes
Because of the ants.
The ants bit him and the bites hurt very much.
The lazy man lost his sleep
Because of the ants.
The lazy man's laziness all went out of him
Because of the ants biting him.
Every day a man does not sleep at his work.
In fact there are many ants at his work.
Long ago the sun turned dust into ants
Because of a lazy man.
Now on earth there are many ants
Because of lazy men.

1971, from a literal version
by Katherine B. Branstetter's
informant Santiago Mendes Zapata

STORY OF THE EATERS

The eaters saddened every heart in Tenejapa.
The eaters couldn't be seen.
The eaters had powers that could murder the souls of people.
The eaters he eats the souls of grown people and children.
The eaters had great powers they could eat the souls of the dead.
The eaters went walking every night to houses because he is looking for
        someone who is open to sickness.
Those who pray and burn candles to God himself
So the eaters won't eat them.
Whoever does not burn candles to God himself

Many eaters come to his house with diseases.
The eaters take souls and lock them up in the low city.
The eaters he gives people vomiting, diarrhea, and headache.
When the eaters lock up souls in the low city
Prayers set them free.
They make prayers for the souls that are locked up.
They pray they burn thirteen candles
Thirteen balls of incense
Five liters of cane alcohol
And one jug of cane wine
And a chicken
And a pack of cigarettes
And four gourds of our tobacco.
Every night the eaters want people. They go to dogs.
If a dog is crying at night like an orphan
The eaters are counting its hairs for it.
The eaters count the dog's hairs when they want people for eating.
If it is not time for the dog's master to die
The dog tells the roosters
It's not time for his master to die
The dog tells the roosters if the eaters come.
"Now you crow," the dog says, "because of my master."
The roosters are always ready
When the eater comes to the dog at night.
If the eater comes to the dog to count the dog's hairs
He stops halfway for a rest counting the dog's hairs.
Then the dog cries like an orphan.
Then when the dog cries like an orphan all the roosters crow.
"Already the place is light.
Let's go now, the roosters are crowing,"
The eater says.
Thus no disease comes to the owners of the houses in Tenejapa.
In fact the dogs and the roosters protect it carefully from eaters.

1971, from a literal version
by Katherine B. Branstetter's
informant Santiago Mendes Zapata

Ants work very much every day none sleep
     in fact they use the daytime
at night they sleep they rest their hearts
     because of their work in the days
when in its time in its season the rain comes
     very much food the ants have gathered
     working in the clear weather
the ants feel no sadness because of the rains
     they feel no hunger with all that food
when the ants went to work in the cloudless season
     the grasshoppers laughed a lot and made fun of them
     why ever should we go to work in fact
     in the clear weather they said
     the grasshoppers making fun of the ants
the grasshoppers did no work in the cornfields every day
     the grasshoppers sleep in the fields
in the nights the grasshoppers have parties
     with their music
all they know how to do at night is have parties with their music
     no work to speak of
the grasshoppers make fun of the ants a lot
     for only working in the cornfields
it came the time of hunger the rainy season for them
     the grasshoppers
none the food of the grasshoppers in the time of the rainy season in fact
     none their work in the clear weather
the grasshoppers suffered with hunger
the grasshoppers came to the ants' houses
won't you lend us some food because we ourselves are dying of hunger
     the grasshoppers said
there is this suffering of yours because there was no work you did
     in the cloudless weather in fact
     in the daytime you slept in the night you had parties the ants said
it is better to work in the clear weather than to be lazy and walk around

and sleep and have parties in the fields
  the ants said to the grasshoppers scolding them
we on the other hand did not sleep in the daytime the ants said
the ants laughed because the grasshoppers
  were suffering from hunger
the grasshoppers were ashamed because the ants had uncovered
  their shame
the grasshoppers began to steal because they were hungry
in the time long ago there were created
  the grasshoppers the creatures who do not work in cornfields
in the time long ago there were created the ants
  who work hard in cornfields

1971, from a literal version
by Katherine B. Branstetter's
informant Santiago Mendes Zapata

Anonymous | Tzotzil
Zinacantan

THE FLOOD

There were still three suns in the sky
And the first people were dwarfs
And the flood came.

And they died
Some died.

And they shut themselves up in coffins
Some.
And they climbed trees
Some.
They broke the stones of fruit with their teeth.
Their meals were acorns
When the world was flooded
At one time.

Well they changed.
Their tails sprouted.
And hair grew on them.
Then they were monkeys.

Well that is how the world ended
At one time.

Then came a change of people.
It was us.

The dwarfs are below.
But often they talk with the gods.

They are tired of it underground.
The sun burns too much there.
They are tired of having nothing but mud to wear.
Mud hats to keep the sun off.

They want to come up here.

So now this world can't last long.

1971, from a version by
Robert Laughlin's informant
Domingo de la Torre P.

BELLY-ACHE

They were in bed together, the woman had a husband, the woman's husband came, spoke with his sister-in-law, talked with her, went to bed with her, didn't know whether there was another, her husband came, his house was closed, he went in to find them, he opened the door, her husband, they are one on top of the other, one on top of his sister-in-law, he wants to kill them, the husband, they changed into birds, they flew away, they went out of the house, they went away until they were on the mountain. One said, "Belly-ache." The other answered, "My sister-in-law, belly-ache." They fly to the mountain. Both of them are crying there now on the mountain.

1971, from a Spanish literal
version by Robert Laughlin's
informant S.A.

Anonymous | Eskimo

THE DREAM

Last night you were in a dream
I dreamed you
walking on the shore
over the little stones
and I was walking with you
last night when I dreamed about you
I dreamed I followed you
I thought I was awake
I wanted you
as though you were a young seal
you were what I wanted
as a young seal
in the eyes of a hunter
before it dives because it's being followed
you were what I wanted
that's how
I wanted you
in my dream about you

1969, from a French version by
Paul-Émile Victor

SONG OF THE OLD WOMAN

A lot of heads around me
a lot of ears around me
a lot of eyes around me
will those ears hear me much longer
will those eyes see me much longer
when those ears don't hear me any more
when those eyes don't look at mine any more
I won't eat liver with blubber any more
then those eyes won't see me any more
and this hair will have disappeared from my head

1969, from a French version by
Paul-Émile Victor

My song was ready
it was in my mouth
it was all ready
my song
but I gave up the hunt
because the sea got rough
the cold North wind blew
and I saw heavy fogs getting up
along the mountain I saw them running
I saw them getting up
the cold wet fogs out of the north sky

1969, from a French version by
Paul-Émile Victor

Bear in mind
regrets
    Andriamatoa

they aren't the man
    who puts his head in the door
    and you say
        Come in

they aren't the man sitting there
    and you say
        Let me get by

they don't give you
    any warning at all
just make fun of you afterward

we can't drive them ahead of us
    like sheep

they follow us
    like dogs

they bounce up
    behind
    like sheep's tails

1970, from the French of
Les Hain-Tenys, by Jean Paulhan

Now you're ripe for me
        and I'm hungry for you

I want to peel you

even if the butterfly brushes you
        the black butterfly
        death

I won't leave you

he who dies for someone he loves
        is a little alligator
        whom his mother swallows

and he finds himself back again
        in the belly he knows so well

1970, from the French of
Les Hain-Tenys, by Jean Paulhan

Anonymous | Malay

MALAY FIGURES

Slow splashing splashing
wakes me
and I cling to the wet pillow

           Stepping on a long thorn
           to me the sight of her hair

I would die
of your fingers
if I could be buried in your palm

           If you go upriver pick me a flower
           if you die before me wait
           just beyond the grave

Daybreak with clouds flying and one star
like a knife in the hill
if I could find her I would see nothing else

           Unless she is the one
           sail on to death
           like an empty ship

The fish line goes out
and out
but one end is in my hand

           Let us row over to the fort crusted with seashells
           even priests sin in spite of their learning
           and what do we know

You knew what I was like
and you started it

> The lime tree bends to the still water
> how sweet your voice is
> when you are thinking of another

If you know a song
sing it

> Setting out for the island
> forget all your clothes
> but not me

1970

KOREAN FIGURES

Even with your aunt
bargain

> You give the child
> you don't like
> one extra

Wash a bean
that's how polished
he seems

> For every beggar
> a day comes
> bringing a guest

Blind
blames the ditch

> Can't see
> steal your own things

Blind horse
follows
bells

> All dressed up
> walking in the dark

I eat the cucumber
my way

Hunchback
is good to
his parents

                        Even on dog turds
                        the dew falls

Chased a chicken
stands looking up

                        A dog with
                        two back doors

Man with ten vices
sneers at the man with one

                        Each finger
                        can suffer

Needle thief
dreams
of spears

                        Quiet
                        like a house where the witch
                        has just stopped dancing

Sparrow shouts
in the teeth of death

                        A gentleman
                        would rather drown
                        than swim dog-paddle

Dress sword
and no pants

Gone like an egg in a river

        Nobody notices hunger
        but nobody misses dirt

Every grave
holds a reason

                1968

Anonymous | Japanese

JAPANESE FIGURES

Autumn rides down
on one leaf

> Autumn
> the deer's
> own color

The world turns
through partings

> Star
> watching
> the day break

Sudden
like a spear from a window

> Feet of the lantern bearer
> move in the dark

Better than the holiday
is the day before

> Departs once
> is forgotten day
> after day

Spits straight up
learns something

When he talks
it clouds the tea

                    Summer rain
                    so hard
                    parted the horse's mane

Blind man
calling his
lost staff

                    Sparrows a hundred years old
                    still dance
                    the sparrow dance

Just got it
in time to lose it

                    If he flatters you
                    watch him

Autumn
glass sky
horses fattening

                    Bird flies up
                    where your foot was going

Wake up
as much as you can

                    Nobody bothers
                    the bad boys

Too big
to be bright all through

Keeps counting up
the dead child's
age

           Death
           collects all the tongues

One god goes
but another comes

           Clouds fly into the moon
           wind full of blossoms

                1970

Anonymous | Chinese

CHINESE FIGURES

One lifetime in office
the next seven lives a beggar

> A judge decides for ten reasons
> nine of which nobody knows

If you get in a fight with a tiger
call your brother

> Before you beat a dog
> find out whose he is

The hissing starts
in the free seats

> For a whole day
> he does nothing
> like the immortals

If two men feed a horse
it will stay thin

> Straightened too much
> crooked as ever

Old man
the sun leaving
the mountain

Rank and position
gulls on water

        Honor
        is brought
        by servants

Wear rags
and the dogs bite

        Let your children
        taste a little cold
        and a little hunger

One word
can warm
the three months of winter

        Don't insult
        those in office
        cheat them

The wind got up in the night
and took our plans away

        So cold
        the cocks crow at midnight

        1969

I have had a companion on the road
we have journeyed shoulder to shoulder
by nature the mountains are green
by nature the water is clear
midnight has passed
this nature is not known
all I hear
is startled monkeys above the monastery

1977, from the French version by
Masumi Shibata

Musō Soseki | Japanese
1275-1351

For years I dug in the earth
trying to discover the blue sky
deeper and deeper I tunnelled
until one night
I made stones and tiles fly into the air
with no effort I broke the bone of the void

1977, from the French version by
Masumi Shibata

Takushitsu | Japanese 1290–1367

A breeze strokes the water of the spring
bringing a cool sound
the moon climbs from the peak in front
lights up the bamboo window frame
With age I have found it good
to be in the heart of the mountains
To die at the foot of a cliff—
the bones would be pure forever

1977, from the French version by
Masumi Shibata

Kalidasa | Sanskrit
5th century A.D.

Even the man who is happy
    glimpses something
    a hair of sound touches him

    and his heart overflows with a longing
        he does not recognize

then it must be that he is remembering
    in a place out of reach
    shapes he has loved

    in a life before this

    the print of them still there in him waiting

1970, translated with
J. Moussaieff Masson

Anonymous | Sanskrit

I like sleeping with somebody
    different

    often

it's nicest when my husband is
    in a foreign country

      and there's rain in the streets at night
      and wind

      and nobody

1970, translated with
J. Moussaieff Masson

Between his hands
Krishna takes
Yasodhā's breast
in his mouth takes
her nipple
at once he remembers
in an earlier life taking
to his mouth the conch shell
to call to battle
all bow down now to
the thought of his skin
at that moment

1971, translated with
J. Moussaieff Masson

Water pouring from clouds
in the night
of palm forests
large ears motionless
they listen
the elephants
eyes half closed
to the sound of the heavy rain
their trunks resting on their tusks

1972, translated with
J. Moussaieff Masson

COSMOLOGY

The goddess Lakshmi
loves to make love to Vishnu
from on top
looking down she sees in his navel
a lotus
and on it Brahma the god
but she can't bear to stop
so she puts her hand
over Vishnu's right eye
which is the sun
and night comes on
and the lotus closes
with Brahma inside

1973, translated with
J. Moussaieff Masson

Hiding in the
cucumber garden
simple country girl shivers
with desire
her lover on a low cot
lies tired with love
she melts into his body
with joy
his neck tight in her arms
one of her feet
flicking a necklace of
seashells hanging
on a vine
on the fence
rattles them to scare off
foxes there in the dark

1973, translated with
J. Moussaieff Masson

Rumi
Persian
1207–1273

The moon which the sky never saw
    even in dreams
    has risen again

    bringing a fire
    that no water can drown

See here where the body
    has its house
    and see here my soul

    the cup of love has made the one
    drunk
    and the other a ruin

When the tavern keeper
    became my heart's companion

    love turned my blood
    to wine
    and my heart burned on a spit

When the eye is full of him
    a voice resounds

      Oh cup
      be praised
      oh wine be proud

Suddenly when my heart saw
    the ocean of love

it leapt away from me calling
    Look for me

The face of Shams-ud Din
    the glory of Tabriz

    is the sun that hearts follow
    like clouds

1974, translated with
Talat Halman

When the heart bursts into flame
    it swallows up
    the believers and the faithless together

    when the bird of truth
    opens its wings
    all the images fly away

The world breaks apart
    the soul is flooded

    the pearl that dissolves into water
    is embraced by the water
    and reborn from the water

The secret appears
    and the forms of the world
    fall away

    suddenly one wave
    is flung upward
    all the way to the green dome of the sky

One moment it's a pen
> one moment it's paper
> one moment it's rapture

> the soul learns to hate
> good and evil
> and keeps stabbing at both

Every soul that reaches God
> enters the majestic
> secret

> turns from a snake
> into a fish

> leaves solid earth
> dives into the sea
> swims in the river of Paradise

The soul moves from earthly bondage
> to the kingdom without place

> after that wherever it falls
> it is bathed in a sea of sweet odor

Absence is also
> divine poverty

> it guides the stars

> the Emperor
> turns to dust on its doorstep
> knocking

Let the glittering surface
> go out

so that the light within
can wake

out of the burning sun
light comes to the heart
to illumine the universe

You are in the service
of the beloved
why are you hiding

you are gold
finer and brighter
at each stroke of the hammer

It is the heart
that sings these words
the wine of eternity
has made it drunk

but these are nothing
to the words it would sing
if it held its breath

1974, translated with
Talat Halman

Wise teacher tell me
who or what do I look like

one minute I'm a phantom
the next I call to the spirits

I stand unscorched and unshrivelled
in the flames of longing
and I am the candle that gives light to everything

I am the smoke and the light I am one
      and I am scattered

The one thing I ever twist in anger
      is the peg of the heart's lyre

the one thing I ever pluck
      with the plectrum
      is the harp of joy

I am like milk and honey
      I strike myself again and again
      I stop myself

when I run mad I rattle my chains

Teacher tell me what kind
      of bird am I
      neither partridge nor hawk

I'm neither beautiful nor ugly
      neither this nor that

I'm neither the peddler in the market
      nor the nightingale
      in the rose garden

Teacher give me a name so that I'll know
      what to call myself

I'm neither slave nor free neither candle
      nor iron

I've not fallen in love with anyone
      nor is anyone in love with me

Whether I'm sinful or good
    sin and goodness come from another
    not from me

Wherever He drags me I go
    with no say in the matter

1977, translated with
Talat Halman

Love you alone have been with us
    since before the beginning of the world

tell us all the secrets one by one
    we are of the same Household as you

In dread of your fire we closed our mouths
    and gave up words

but you are not fire
    you are without flames

Moment by moment
    you destroy the city of the mind

gust of wind to the mind's candle
    wine for the fire-worshippers

Friend with friends
    enemy with enemies

or somewhere between the two
    looking for both

To the sane
    the words of lovers are nothing but stories

if that was all you were
how could you turn night into day

You whose beauty sends the world reeling
your love brings about all this confusion

You are that love's masterpiece
you make it clear

O sun of God
sultan of sultans
glory and joy of Tabriz

you give light to those on earth
beauty and splendor of the age

1977, translated with
Talat Halman

If you're not going to sleep
sit up
I've already slept

go on and tell your story
I've finished mine

I've finished that story
because I'm tired

lurching the way drunks do
staggering
ready to pass out

Asleep or awake
I'm thirsty
for the beloved

my companion
    my cherished friend
    is the image
    of the beloved

Like the mirror
    I exist only because
    of that face

for whose sake
    I display features
    or hide them

When the image of the beloved smiles
    I smile
    when the image stirs and rages with passion

I stir and rage too
    with passion
    I too let go

For the rest
    why don't you
    tell it
    you

each of the pearls
    after all
    that I'm piercing and stringing together

    came out of your sea

1977, translated with
Talat Halman

Yunus Emré | Turkish
died ca. 1320

The whole universe is full of God
      yet His truth is seen by no one
      you have to look for Him in yourself
      you and He are not separate you are one

The other world is what can't be seen
      here on earth we must live as well as we can
      exile is grieving and anguish
      no one comes back who has once gone

Come let us be friends this one time
      let life be our friend
      let us be lovers of each other
      the earth will be left to no one

You know what Yunus is saying
      its meaning is in the ear of your heart
      we should all live truly here
      for we will not live here forever

1977, translated with
Talat Halman

Mirza Ghalib | Urdu 1797–1869

GHAZAL V

The drop dies in the river
of its joy
pain goes so far it cures itself

in the spring after the heavy rain the cloud
disappears
that was nothing but tears

in the spring the mirror turns green
holding a miracle
Change the shining wind

the rose led us to our eyes

let whatever is be open

1968, translated with Aijaz Ahmad

GHAZAL XII

I am not a flower of song
        nor any of the bright shuttles of music
I am the sound of my own breaking

You think of how your hair looks
I think of the ends of things

We think we know our own minds
but our hearts are children

Now that you have appeared to me I bow
may you be blessed

You look after the wretched
no wonder you came
        looking for me

1968, translated with Aijaz Ahmad

GHAZAL XV

Almost none
of the beautiful faces
come back to be glimpsed for an instant in some flower

once the dust owns them

The three Daughters of the Bier
as becomes stars
hide in the light till day has gone

then they step forth naked
but their minds are the black night

He is the lord of sleep
lord of peace
lord of night

on whose arm your hair is lying

1968, translated with Aijaz Ahmad

GHAZAL XXI

Red poppy
     a heart
     an eye

       one dewdrop on it
       a tear

       there to hide something

       she is cruel
       it leaves its mark

But the scar of the burnt heart
     oh my cry
     is nothing

       beside you oh my cry
       dove
       turned to ashes
       nightingale
       prison of color

No blaze of meeting
     could have burned like the longing to meet

       the spirits were consumed
       the heart suffered torture

If a man claims to be a prisoner of love
     he is a prisoner of something
     hand held down by a stone
     faithful

O sun

      you light the whole world
      here also
      shine

      a strange time has come over us
      like a shadow

1968, translated with Aijaz Ahmad

GHAZAL XXV

If ever it occurs to her to be kind to me
      she remembers how cruel she's been
      and it frightens her off

Her temper's as short as my tale of love is long
      much too long
      bores even the messenger

      and I despair
      and lose the thread of my own thoughts

      and can't bear to think of someone else
      setting eyes on her

1968, translated with Aijaz Ahmad

GHAZAL XXXIV

He's going around with your letter
showing
would be happy to read it out

Kind as she is she's made so fine
I'd be afraid to touch her
if she'd let me

Death will come whether I wait for her or not
I ask you to come whether I want you
or not

The vision
hangs before the Divine like a curtain
whose is it

Helpless with the fire of love
Ghalib
can't light it can't put it out

1968, translated with Aijaz Ahmad

Selected Translations
1978–2011

CONTENTS 1978–2011

This foreword was begun as an introduction to the third volume of selected translations representing the translations I have done over the past thirty years. I soon realized that it should be an attempt to place in perspective my whole lifetime as a translator, and the ideas and ideals of translation itself that have evolved since I began, over sixty years ago, to work at this unfinishable art.

~

More than once during the years that are represented by this selection, I had persuaded myself that I had finished trying to translate poetry. It was a moment whose time seemed to have come. Yet I kept finding that I had been led back again, sometimes by a suggestion from someone else, other times by something—perhaps a single line or phrase—that suddenly caught me in the original, maybe a line or phrase with which I had long been familiar. This indecisiveness, I realize, is quite consistent with the impossible art of translating, for there is no such thing as the final translation of a poem. Only the original is unique and absolute: it essentially cannot exist "in other words." And one part of the impossibility of translating any poem is the fact that what we want the translation to be is exactly what it never can be, the original. Yet the impossibility of the whole enterprise is part of the perennial temptation to try again.

This magnetic attraction came to seem "natural" to me, as habits tend to do. It seemed to have grown there on its own, a native. It must have been rooted in my early fascination with the sound of language, which I am convinced is innate in every human. In societies with strong oral traditions this fascination is taken for granted. When I became aware of it I was too young to try to describe it even to myself. I remember being intrigued by phrases with an unfamiliar sound—in poems that my mother read to my sister and me, and in hymns that were sung, above my head in church (my father was a Presbyterian minister): the sound of Tennyson's brook babbling, babbling as it went to join the brimming river, and the spacious firmament on high, and all the blue ethereal sky... which seemed to have a dimension and clarity of their own to me, though the actual words did not. One day before I went to school—so before my fourth birthday—my father took me to the church with him, a block away, where he rehearsed Sunday's sermon. I was to sit very still and listen. My father did not often ask me to come along with him when he went out, and it was something of an occasion for me. First he read from the scripture, from the sixth chapter of the book of Isaiah. My father, I am happy to say, always read in the King James Version, and I heard, in the empty church:

> In the year that king Uzziah died I saw also the Lord sitting upon a throne, high and lifted up, and his train filled the temple.
> Above it stood the seraphims: each one had six wings; with twain he covered his face, and with twain he covered his feet, and with twain he did fly...

Not even in my father's previous readings from the pulpit did I remember ever having heard language like that, and it rang in my ears. I wanted to hear that sound again, and to hear more of the life in the words, though I had only a remote sense of what the words meant, as I did sometimes when my mother read poems or fairy tales to us. As we walked home I kept trying to remember phrases, mumbling them to myself under my breath. (My father and I were not conversing as we walked. We seldom did, unless he was telling me not to do something. I realized eventually that he had no idea of how to be a father. He was the youngest, by several years, of seven children, but he had never seen much of his own father, who was away most of the time on the river. But somewhere, either from my grandmother's reading the scriptures aloud, or from the Rimerton village church, on the hill above the railroad tracks, my father had picked up a love of the sound of language. It was the sound more or less apart from the meaning, as I came to see. For him, I think, the function of words in public was almost entirely rhetorical. He had little judgment, and though he loved to quote to himself phrases such as *For every beast of the forest is mine*, and *the cattle upon a thousand hills*, he betrayed at times a similar fondness for maudlin rhetoric. He was not at all literary or intellectual. I do not remember his ever reading a whole book, or anything except the local papers and bits from such magazines as came into the house. He had no ear for music either, and said so. His own use of language was vague and indolent. He seldom finished a sentence. Yet his sensitivity to the sound of language, to some magic in what he had heard there, was genuine, and he never lost that. I am grateful to him for my having heard a bit of that magic, so early.)

Some distant variant of the sound that I had heard in the church, that morning, I heard in poems my mother read to us. There was a gentle echo of it in Stevenson's "Where Go the Boats." It was part of my growing fascination with language itself: in phrases heard out on the street, in slang, and of course in words that I was told were forbidden. When I learned to read (from a book about "Indians" who did not read or write), I went on listening.

Some years later, after my family had moved to Scranton, Pennsylvania, and I was attending West Scranton Junior High School, as it was then called, I chose the classical curriculum and began to study Latin, with a very competent and exacting teacher. I realize now how lucky I was to be able to start there, and also, of course, how much finer public education was in those years just before World War II. Homework assignments and tests included translations of paragraphs of Caesar's *Gallic Wars*. The focus was entirely on Latin grammatical forms, and corresponding phrases in English, and the course ignored the smooth self-serving ruthlessness of the account itself with its appalling series of events; the *Gallic Wars* combined personal megalomania and an unquestioning imperialism in an attitude that would remain essential to the history of Europe for centuries to come, and it would be some years before I began to realize its real, and devastating, nature. In the meantime, the close attention to another language, and to making lumbering translations of one of its classics, led me after class to try to translate common phrases of contemporary English into Latin. It turned into a habit, a kind of private game that I would play while I was doing some household chore—sweeping the long porches, or weeding under the hedge along the front sidewalk. I persisted with more malleable material, a couple of years later, when at another school I began to learn Spanish from a man whom I still consider a great teacher, Laurence Sampson, a man who had a passion for the language and culture of Spain, and for life itself, although he was aging rapidly and would soon die. By the time I knew him he could climb a flight of stairs only by resting every two or three steps and clutching the banister while he caught his breath. He bore it all with a lightness and a turn of wit that I was not used to hearing from my generally humorless elders. (As I think of him, that wit and his broad view and love of the world seem to me inseparable from his moustache, twirled into points.) I am indebted to him for enlivening and extending my early delight in language. My love of Spanish is a legacy from him.

Going to Princeton on a scholarship was a great, exciting expansion of horizons. I arrived there toward the end of World War II when civilian classes were small, and there was the great library with its open stacks. I went on studying Spanish. My new teacher was a very homesick young man from Spain, named Soria, who wore a black beret, pulled down around his head, and rode a bicycle everywhere. (No cars were allowed on the quiet campus in those days.) His homesickness fed a passion for the writing of Federico García Lorca, whose plays he wanted to translate, but his English was not adequate, and he asked a few of us to help him. I enjoyed our work together and obediently shared his enthusiasm for Lorca's plays, or tried to, but it was Lorca's poems, which we read with him, that I really loved, especially the *Romancero gitano* and the *Poema del cante jondo*. Lorca was the first modern poet I read. I tried to translate some of his poems with Professor Soria's help, lured by the opening lines of one of Lorca's ballads, "The Unfaithful Bride":

> *Y que yo me la llevé al río*
> *creyendo que era mozuela,*
> *pero tenía marido.*

> And so I brought her down to the river
> believing she was a maiden,
> but she had a husband.

That was the meaning, but the result in English was dull and flat, and I could not imagine how to convey the power and daring and grace of the original, the passion and dance movement that were the very spirit of those lines. I realized that if ever I could approach anything of the kind, it would make translating that poem—it would make translation itself—worth doing. I could see that the word *translation* was not the simple replication that it suggested, but that translation included a whole range of possible representations. Literal versions obviously were indispensable, yet it was not the flat literal transcription that I aspired to produce but something harder to describe, even to myself.

It was around that time that William Arrowsmith, who was an older student, a friend of mine, enthusiastically showed me some of the poetry of Wallace Stevens. (The only poets I had been reading in the English language, besides Shakespeare, were Milton and Shelley.) I began to haunt the Parnassus Bookshop, where other students who were discovering modern poetry hung out. The bookshop occupied the two front rooms of a little nineteenth-century house half a block north of Washington Road, on Nassau Street. What had been the living room—with a small black marble fireplace, an ormolu clock on the mantel—and the dining room behind it had been turned into the bookshop. Keene and Anne Fleck, who lived upstairs, had opened the shop, lining the walls with bookshelves, and they had their meals and sat with visitors around the table in the kitchen, down the hall. Their shop specialized in poetry and philosophy—but above all poetry—and I spent most of my tiny allowance on books that I found there. And those were treasures, from Wyatt and Surrey and Fulke Greville and Chapman to Ezra Pound's *Personae*. It was the American, New Directions edition, reprinted from the 1926 English, Boni & Liveright edition, and it contained Pound's selection of all his poems written before the Cantos, and of his translations, from T'ang Chinese, Latin, and "Provençal," as the language of the troubadours was called then. I put down my $3.50—the price on the jacket flap—and before I left the store I had discovered a new sound in poetry in the English language, a sound that was even clearer in some of the translations than in many of Pound's own poems. At the same moment, without realizing it, I had stepped into one of the insoluble enigmas of modern poetry in English. I did not learn about it immediately, but it was not long before someone told me that Pound had been arrested by the American army, in Italy, and charged with treason for broadcasting on Italian radio in support of Mussolini, in wartime, and for that there had been army officers who wanted to have him shot. I was told that he had been saved by a Quaker lawyer using a plea of insanity, and that Pound, in accord with the sentence, had been locked up in a psycho ward of an American military hospital in Washington, D.C.

At first this was all I knew about Pound, and none of my friends seemed to know any more. Though profoundly excited by what I was reading and discovering with the guidance of my professors at Princeton and on my own, I was riding an undercurrent of rebellion toward conventional authority in general, and against my own upbringing and background. Sticking out one's tongue at those in authority did not seem such a terrible thing, and what I had heard about his offense sounded foolish—but hardly more serious than that. I was prejudiced on Pound's behalf, because he had become a kind of hero to me. A young man from very humble origins, whose father was a dirt farmer on a small homestead plot in central Idaho in the last decades of the nineteenth century, Ezra had decided in early youth to become a poet, and he had managed to do it. That was what I wanted to do, and I was encouraged by his example when I read about him. The encouragement seemed to be borne out by the utterly original voice I heard in his poems and translations.

The following spring, after I had turned nineteen, a college friend invited me to his family's house in D.C. during the Easter vacation, and I telephoned St. Elizabeth's, the military hospital where Pound was incarcerated, asking to visit him. They consented, and he consented.

I was led in through a locked, ironclad door to a large shabby room that seemed to have been made by knocking out partitions between a series of smaller ones. It had all been painted a grayish green at some point in the past. Into the walls had been cut insets and alcoves. I was led into one of the larger areas, around the corner from the entrance door. Heavy metal grids lined the tall windows. I was shown to a chair, and Pound, a moment later, was led in. He greeted me with a friendly laugh and we sat facing each other. He was sixty-one, but he looked older to me. Thin, rather gaunt, his hair and the pointed beard gray. When he laughed he threw his head back, revealing rows of gold teeth. He made no reference to his circumstances, ignoring one of the inmates, in pajamas, who walked slowly up and down the length of the room, pausing to pull what seemed to be an imaginary chain, maybe a toilet chain. Pound said, "So you're a poet." I told him that I hoped so. He nodded as though he were taking that under serious consideration, and he asked whether I had read any of his cantos. I said only the first few, and he began to tell me about the plan for their final form, when the last cantos would complete the original design, holding all the others in place, like the frieze over the top of a row of columns—he mimed with his hands what he meant.

He returned before long to the subject of my own aspirations, and I explained more or less how they had led me to him. He nodded like a teacher and proceeded to talk to me as though he took my words seriously. I realized then and later that he loved the role of the pedagogue. Pound, Gertrude Stein had said, "was a village explainer, excellent if you were a village…" Some of the advice he gave me as we sat there was unforgettable and has been valuable to me ever since. He said, "If you're going to be a poet you have to take it seriously and work at it every day. Try to write seventy-five lines a day. Now, at your age, you don't have anything to write seventy-five lines about, even if you think you do. So the thing to do is to get languages and translate." He asked me what languages I knew and I said a bit of Spanish, after a bit of high school Latin. He nodded and took it in without comment, and then he said, "The Spanish is all right. Get the *romancero*. Those poems, the oldest ones, are closest to the source. But best of all is the Provençal. Try to get the Provençal. Those troubadours wrote closest to the music. They heard the music before the words sometimes, and sometimes they wrote the music, too. The translation of it is not simple, but trying to do it will be the best teacher you will ever find. Translating will teach you your own language."

I have found that to be true, through the years that I have spent trying to make translations. His words confirmed conclusions that I came to as I worked. For example, I believe that a translation should in some way be stretching English, making it accommodate something new to it, a usage it had never quite had before. It should be making, however unnoticeably, something new.

Pound said to me, "Try to get as close to the original as possible." That sounded simple. I thought I knew what he meant until I tried to put it into practice. His own example did little to clarify the matter. He was not a scholar of either Occitan (the Provençal) or T'ang Chinese, and there were misspellings and vagaries in some of the troubadour poems. And in what was probably his best-known and most influential translation, that of Li Po's "The River-Merchant's Wife: A Letter"—the first line of which seems to have echoed in the ears of most of the English-language poets since it was first published—he edited and rearranged and abbreviated the poem (as freely as he would do with the complete draft of *The Waste Land* when Eliot showed it to him). The line is: "While my hair was still cut straight across my forehead," and certainly it does not seem as revolutionary now, more than a century later, as it must have seemed when it appeared, in an age where the conventional run-of-the-mill poetry droned on in its somnolent post-Tennysonian pentameter. Pound's translations, and Arthur Waley's translations from the same "Golden Age" of Chinese poetry, have had a crucial effect on poetry in English, particularly American poetry. In Pound's translations—if that is what they should be called—of the Latin poet Sextus Propertius, he had completely recast and rewritten those passages of the original from which his own versions were made. Yet none of that was really as revolutionary a practice as it may have seemed. Sir Thomas Wyatt's great poem that begins, "Whoso list to hunt, I know where is an hind," had its origin in a sonnet of Petrarch's, all but unrecognizable (and never acknowledged) in Wyatt's powerful lines. Ben Jonson's peerless lyric, "Drink to me only with thine eyes," was fashioned out of parts of two short Latin poems written, if the ascriptions are correct, by two different poets of the "Silver Age" of Latin poetry. One of the pillars of Victorian poetry is Edward FitzGerald's "Rubáiyát of Omar Khayyám"—a free adaptation and remaking of the original, which some critics who know the original have considered a misrepresentation. There seem to be almost as many precedents for such innovation as there are memorable translations. But Pound's advice to try to get as close as possible to the original remained, although I am not sure, all these years later, what he meant when he said it. It was still good advice, a basic aspiration to keep returning to.

I had it in mind as I tried to translate a medieval poem written in what is now Old French, by Richard the Lion Heart. I had come upon the poem in a course in Old French that was the closest thing to the Provençal that was available, when I went back to Princeton after the meeting with Pound. (The university apparently did not want to waste a full-sized classroom on the handful of students mumbling over Old French texts, under the guidance of a tiny French scholar as dry as a winter leaf.) I knew so little of the original poem's context that I did not recognize the poem as a real troubadour poem, composed in the French of the time, rather than in Provençal, in order to make it more readily accessible to Richard's powerful captor. In the course of my studies I managed to produce a labored translation of it, which was one of the first translations I published, in the first issue of the *Hudson Review*, in 1948.

When I had come back to Princeton after that spring visit, I had also taken to heart Pound's advice about "the Spanish" and the *romancero*. The word means, roughly, "ballad collection," and after I browsed happily for a while in the open stacks of the great library, it looked to me like a fairly comprehensive collection. After thumbing through it, I picked, more or less at random, one from the earliest section, a poem whose opening words were *descolorida zagala*, which means, literally, "pale maiden" or "faded maiden," and I struggled for some weeks trying to make out of those words something with life and music to it. This was an important lesson to me in choosing what poems to try or not to try to translate, and that poem was one that my friend Clarence Brown, years later, would have described as a poem that "loses a lot in the original."

Pound continued to send me penciled notes, mostly on postcards, with nuggets of advice. The most memorable of them read, in its entirety, "Read seeds not twigs EP." I went on trying to translate ancient, and also modern, poems from Spanish, and continued to try to "get" what Pound called the Provençal. After I finished at Princeton, a job as a tutor with an American family who had a house in France took me to Europe. One tutoring job led to another: the second one took me to Portugal, where I tried to translate some Portuguese medieval poetry linked to the troubadours north of the Pyrenees. At the same time, of course, I was trying to write poems of my own. The following summer, wandering, with almost no money, in Spain, I went to Mallorca, hoping to meet Robert Graves. I had no introduction, but found my way to his house in the mountain village of Deya. He welcomed me and he arranged for me to stay in the village, in the former palace of the secretary of Louis Salvador, second cousin of Emperor Franz Joseph of Austria. Louis Salvador himself had lived for most of his adult life in another palace, out along the cliffs of the coast on the way to Valldemossa. Robert Graves asked me to edit one of the appendixes that he was adding to a new, expanded edition of *The White Goddess*, the section on birds, and while I was doing that he received a letter from England, from the young man whom Robert was expecting to come to Mallorca as a tutor to Robert and Beryl's older son, William. The letter brought news that the young man would not be coming after all, and so Robert offered me the job, "if I would leave the Portuguese job." The choice was not easy, but I travelled back (on milk trains, for my salaries as a tutor were minimal) to Portugal and broke the news, and parted with my employer there, Princess Maria Antonia da Braganza, and then travelled back to Mallorca and my third tutoring job.

The year in Deya, working in the same very small, ancient village up on the cliffs, introduced me to a whole new perspective on history, antiquity, tradition, and poetry, and to another life dedicated to all of these. For me they were a confirmation. After the year working with Robert, and some time in London, I returned to the village for another winter and worked there translating the *Poem of the Cid* for the BBC Third Programme. Other translations commissioned for the Third Programme—including *The Song of Roland*, classical Spanish plays by Lope de Vega, and programs of contemporary American and English poetry—were the main source of my livelihood for the time I was in London, and the translations for the BBC were valuable practice. While I was in London, in 1952, my first book of poems was published in the Yale Younger Poets series.

I continued to translate poetry, modern and ancient, including poems by Neruda and other Spanish and French poets as I discovered them. Troubadour poems, including the poem in Old French, were song lyrics, which are always especially hard to translate if the translator tries to convey their rhythmic and musical quality. Pound had called their original language Provençal, as most people would have done at that time. But the origins of the troubadour tradition, and so of the entire Romance tradition, were in fact far to the west of the region that the Romans had called Provence, meaning the province of the Empire beyond the Alps. The first great gathering place of the earliest troubadours was in the château of Ventadorn (in modern French Ventadour) in what is now the mountainous *département* of the Corrèze, south of Limoges. The first generations of troubadours, most of them of noble birth, came from the Aquitaine, a large area that includes Poitiers, Toulouse, Bordeaux. The region was utterly devastated in the following century, the thirteenth, by the carnage and looting of the Albigensian Crusade and the Hundred Years' War that followed it. The name Provençal has come to be used, most often, for the revival of the language and, to some degree, of its poetic usages, a movement whose principal representative was the poet Mistral. The earlier troubadour language is now generally called Occitan, though that is not an ideal name either, for it may be a French way of indicating the tongue in which they say *oc* to mean "yes," instead of *oui*, as the French do north of the Loire. We really do not know what name those troubadours used for their own language, or indeed whether they felt the need to give it a name at all. They may have referred to it, as Guilhem de Peitau did of the languages of birdsong, as *lor lati*, "their own Latin."

I went on reading, listening for the sound of poetry wherever I could find it, in the original languages and in translations, from Milton's incomparable echo of an ode of Horace's, to Frances Desmore's utterly plain versions of the arrowlike lyrics of the native inhabitants of the nineteenth-century American West. As my horizon expanded like the view of a morning field when the clouds withdraw, the original remained as desirable, as indispensable but as elusive as ever.

By the late fifties I was back in the States again, for the winters, first in Boston and then in the Lower East Side of New York, but spending the summers in an ancient farming village I had found by chance, in part of southern France near where the troubadour tradition had first flowered. I had fallen in love with a ruined farmhouse at the edge of a hamlet, on a ridge overlooking the whole valley of the upper Dordogne river. The building had not been inhabited since the early years of the century, and when I found the woman who owned it she agreed—though only after long hesitation—to sell it to me for the exact tiny sum I had inherited from a maiden aunt, a schoolteacher, but she sold it only on condition that I "would live in it" and not just turn around and sell it again. The house, the old farm buildings, the elders of the ancient village became a pole of my life and also a doorway to the beginnings of the troubadour, and to the entire Romance tradition.

By the late fifties and early sixties there was a kind of seismic shift among American poets of my generation, one that has received considerable attention since that time from reviewers and literary historians. It has been described, sometimes, as though there had been some kind of committee meeting at which we had all agreed to take unprecedented paths. Nothing of the sort happened, of course. Probably the first public—deliberately public—manifestation that something was new was the appearance, in San Francisco, of the Beats. A few literary journalists began to analyze the new generation of poets as though they were announcing a ball game: *The Beats against the Academics!* It was too simple and simple-minded from the start, even though the counterculture that the Beats were happy to represent was prone to a superior and somewhat aggressive manner. The manner itself was enough for some of them, but the generation was made up of individuals, and individual talents, and one of the sources of its adventurous development was a growing interest in the poetry of languages other than English, including nonliterate languages. This included, from the start, new attempts to translate poetry from traditions wholly distinct from the corpus of poetry in English, and to expand the possible meanings of the word *translation* and the practice of translating. Robert Bly, James Wright, Jerome Rothenberg, Michael Benedikt, Philip Levine immediately come to mind. Among our elders, Robert Lowell and Randall Jarrell were carried by the same wave. Projects were formed encouraging freedom that verged on impressionism, in translating from cultures unknown to the conventions of English. I contributed, along with a number of other contemporary poets, to a volume of "translations" of the ghazals of Mirza Ghalib, guided by a bilingual Pakistani poet, Aijaz Ahmad, for whom the original Urdu was a native language. He sought an impressionistic freedom in representing Ghalib.

During that decade I came to feel increasingly discontented with the way the word *translation* had come to be used with growing carelessness in relation to source material. Some of us began to use other designations: *versions, adaptations,* and so on. Robert Lowell called some of his derivations "imitations." Again, Pound was a precursor. When he had published his English passages from the Latin poet Sextus Propertius he had called the whole work "Homage to Sextus Propertius." Lowell had considered the matter in his own earlier books. In *Lord Weary's Castle,* published in the forties, one poem of several pages is derived from passages of the elegies of Propertius, to whom "the ghost" of Propertius's dead mistress, Cynthia, addresses the poem.

But I came to the conclusion that the word *translation* should be more responsibly used, to represent as clearly as possible some aspects of the original. I went on translating poems from the French of Jean Follain, and from the Spanish of Jaime Sabines and Pablo Neruda, and they were more obviously translations in a conventional sense, conveying whatever I was able to evoke of the sense of life of the original words.

In the seventies, when I had settled on the island of Maui, a visiting professor from Japan, named Sōiku Shigematsu, who taught American literature in his native country, especially the Transcendentalists, Emerson and Thoreau, spent several weeks on Maui. He suggested that he and I collaborate in translating the poems of Musō Soseki (1275–1351), a Zen teacher (the title *soseki* means "teacher of the emperor"). Musō was an enormously talented man. Some of his poems are still chanted (or they were a generation ago) in Rinzai rituals in some temples; besides which, he was one of the greatest of all Japanese garden designers, and was a sought-after teacher of kendo, the art of swordsmanship, though he never touched a sword. Shigematsu-san's father was a Rinzai Zen priest with a small, ancient, very beautiful temple in rural western Japan. Shigematsu-san had grown up hearing Musō's poems chanted in the temple. When he sent me his English literal versions of the poems, they were arranged on the page with the phrases in the order in which they had been chanted, and in working on the translations we tried to echo that order in English. Shigematsu-san had studied English all through his school and university years and had also studied Zen as a young man. He and I collaborated, sporadically, through draft after draft, for almost ten years, and I added translations I made from Musō's prose—a single book of letters, called *Dialogues in a Dream*, answering a hundred questions from the former emperor of Japan. I translated the prose from an edition in French by a Rinzai master, Masumi Shibata, who was teaching in France.

During the years when we were working together I visited Shigematsu-san and his father's temple, where his father had a tangerine orchard, and I loved to watch him walking among his trees in his black robes, pruning the branches.

Around 1990 Daniel Halpern wrote to invite me to contribute to a translation project that he was beginning to assemble, asking a number of poets to translate two cantos each of Dante's *Inferno*. I told him that I had said for years that there were degrees in the impossibility of translating poetry, and that Dante, the real, unique life of Dante's *Commedia*, could not be conjured into English. Dan did not take that for an answer, but said, "Take a while to consider." Then he baited the hook by saying, "If you did decide to do it, which cantos would you choose?"

As I pondered Dan's question, I thought of a passage in the twenty-sixth canto of the *Inferno*, which I had read in translation when I was eighteen, and which had seized me then and led me into the rest of Dante, and to the Temple Classics volumes I carried, for years, in my pockets. It was Odysseus's speech, his reply to Virgil, out of the flame he shares with Diomedes, drifting in the dark void. Virgil had asked him where he had gone to die, after his return to Ithaca, and the voice said that nothing, not his love for his wife nor for his son nor for his kingdom and his native place, could keep him contented in Ithaca, and that he had assembled a crew of his old comrades-in-arms and set out to sail farther, exploring parts of the world that were still unknown to them. They had voyaged as far as the western end of the Mediterranean and "those pillars," he said, "which Hercules had set up as landmarks" warning humans to go no farther. There, the voice said, he had turned to his crew and made the speech that had mesmerized me when I first read it in translation. The words, in Dante's Italian, began:

Io e ' compagni eravam vecchi e tardi

In the Temple Classics edition, the John Aitken Carlyle translation read: "I and my companions were old and tardy," and from the beginning I wondered about that "tardy." While I was still a student I read the John D. Sinclair translation (Oxford, 1939) in which the word is translated "slow." I was dubious about that word, too. "Slow" and "tardy" were literal renderings, but it seemed to me that they missed a point of Odysseus's (and so too of Dante's) speech. In 1970 the Charles S. Singleton translation, a masterful work of scholarly research, was published, and again the word was "slow." Each time that I had read the translations and had taken my doubts away with me, I had done no more than that, since I did not intend to try to make a translation of my own. But this time I paused to consider how I might translate it myself. I felt sure that "tardy" was not Dante's principal meaning for the word, although Odysseus and his companions had already spent years growing up, starting families, becoming part of the expedition to Troy and the years in Troy, and then the years of returning to their homelands, before joining the present expedition. I could not believe that "slow" was really what he meant at all. What indication was there in the *Iliad* or the *Odyssey* that they had ever been "slow"? I thought the point was not "late" in the sense of being "late for dinner," but of having "reached their later years," and I considered

I and my companions were old and near the end

and I went on to see how I would finish the line, and how it worked
with the lines that followed. I was already caught, and I undertook to
see whether I could, for Daniel Halpern's volume, make versions of that
canto and of the one that followed.

Dante's Odysseus and his story had remained, for me, one of the most
magnetic passages in the *Inferno*. I learned that Dante is believed not to
have read the Homeric poems themselves but to have known the clas-
sical account of Odysseus/Ulysses from Virgil and perhaps other Latin
sources. His tale of Odysseus is probably his own invention. It made of
Odysseus, it has been said, one of the first modern figures, one who makes
history with a degree of independence of the past, and pursues knowledge
for its own sake, beyond reference to precedent or previous authority.
The eagerness of the fictional Dante, the protagonist of the *Commedia*, to
converse with the ghost of this fictional Odysseus is so intense that Virgil
fears that the figure he is guiding may fall into the abyss, and draws him
back. The Odysseus of Dante's invention is the rare—and perhaps sole—
figure whom Dante meets in that closed, immutable realm who has had a
vision—though a fatal one—of Mount Purgatory, and Odysseus ends his
last story telling of his one glimpse of that mountain. Dante's use of numer-
ology, among his tools for planning that most minutely planned of mas-
terpieces, led me to look for links between that canto and the twenty-sixth
canto of the *Purgatorio*, another canto that I have loved since I first read it.
The theme of the latter canto is carnal love contrasted with love in the form
of generosity beyond selfishness and vanity, and Dante's avatars are art-
ists—poets whom Dante regards as his ancestors and greets with profound
reverence. Each of these in turn points out to him another figure, telling
Dante that the other one had been a greater poet. It is from this sequence
that T.S. Eliot took the phrase (*il miglior fabbro*) with which he dedicated
The Waste Land to Ezra Pound, thereby calling Pound the "*miglior fabbro del
parlar materno*"—the finest workman in the mother tongue. The "mother
tongue" is, of course, poetry itself, but for Dante it would also have been
the language of the troubadours, whatever Dante would have called it.

The line refers to the figure in whom the canto reached its cul-
mination: Arnaut Daniel, whom Dante revered as the greatest of the

troubadours, his ancestral figures. Daniel's reply, with which the canto ends, is not in Italian but in Arnaut Daniel's own language, the *lati* of the troubadours. Dante could have paid him no deeper tribute. And in Daniel's answer the poet addresses Dante as someone who is on his way "to the top of the stair," to the highest realm, the Paradise which he himself hopes to see when his time comes. It is never clear, from Dante's portrayal of Daniel, whether the troubadour's purgation was suffered for physical indulgence in carnal lust or merely for the glorification of erotic love and longing, which was the great central theme of the troubadours. Daniel's reference to "the top of the stair," like the words of Odysseus describing his final glimpse of Mount Purgatory, convey a vision of a life beyond, another world, indeed another dimension, for in the *Purgatorio* there is the dimension of hope, which was absent by eternal decree from the *Inferno*. That may be the link, or part of the link, between the two cantos number XXVI.

When I had sent versions of the two *Inferno* cantos to Daniel Halpern, I looked to see what I could do with the *Purgatorio*. From its beginning until the disappearance of Virgil, near its end, it had always been my favorite part of the *Commedia*. It is the section of the poem that includes Dante's love of music, song, and poetry. I had wondered for years how the first generations of troubadours had come to be as familiar as they were with the Welsh Arthurian legends. At the time of the Norman invasion of Britain, the Welsh had sided with the invaders, against their own perennial enemy, the Teutonic people, Danes and "Anglo-Saxons," who had invaded Britain in waves that began centuries before the Normans arrived. The origins of Welsh poetry, or at least the earliest Welsh poems that survive, tell of an early, temporarily decisive battle between Welsh warriors and the Teutonic invaders. As the legends of that battle grew, the first poems about it that are now known—Aneirin's brief elegies for the already legendary warriors who had died there—became the embryo of the legends of Arthur and the Round Table. (The etymological root of Arthur means "the Bear.") The historic Arthur, by the time of Aneirin's poems, had already become a semidivine archetype, but in his lifetime Arthur had indeed fought the Anglo-Saxons to a standstill.

The Arthurian legends, and perhaps some of the unique power of their language, in both poetry and prose, apparently became a welcome entertainment in the Norman courts, first in Britain and then in Normandy and the Occitan culture to the south. There must have been numerous storytellers and bards, with a body of glorious tales and poems. Jessica Weston in her seminal book *From Ritual to Romance* (1908), from which Eliot drew the figure of the Fisher King, tells of one such travelling bard and storyteller, but he must have been one of many. One of the earliest troubadours, Bernart de Ventadorn, addressed his *jongleur*, his singer, as Tristan, a name from a Celtic *romance*. There is a legend that the book Paolo and Francesca were reading on the day when they "read no more forever," was a lost romance by Arnaut Daniel. But most of the Occitan romances did not survive; probably one more legacy of the Albigensian Crusade and the Hundred Years' War. Their stories were carried north to the French culture beyond the Loire, and were incorporated in the great French romances of the next centuries. They were the source of the tales in the romances of Chrétien de Troyes, and from there they travelled, in French, back to Britain.

The last of the Middle English romances that arose from that returning wave was *Sir Gawain and the Green Knight*, and it is one of the greatest of them all. It carries within it echoes of its ancient Welsh origins and accretions from its continental wanderings. There are learned, meticulous translations that reproduce, word by word, the alliterative form of the original, and I have paid close and respectful attention to them (Marie Boroff's above all). But the alliterative pattern, which was the convention used by the unknown original author, sounds wearisome to us, and I wanted to see whether I could get closer to a rhythmic sound that would keep the audience, for I was assuming that the original audiences listened, before they read—if they could read at all. I remembered, and tried to listen to, two echoes. One echo was the Welsh language and the Welsh accent in English that I had grown up hearing in the coal-mining town of Scranton. The other was the work, above all the late fragments, of David Jones, whom I think of as the greatest overlooked poet in English in the twentieth century. I reread the *Gawain* trying to hear whether those echoes seemed to have anything to do with it, and I thought they did.

Only scholars of the archaic language can read the provincial or pre-Chaucerian Middle English now, and the version I produced is an attempt to bring into our hearing some of the original excitement of the story. I felt certain it was something that would have to be audible, whether or not it was ever actually read aloud, for I was sure that many of those who first came to it were illiterate.

In the years since the *Gawain* was published I have continued to try to translate some troubadour poems, and have translated poems from French and Spanish, including a book-length selection of the work of the Mexican poet Jaime Sabines, whose poems I have loved for decades.

The one collection, in recent years, that has grown into something more extensive is the still untitled complete poems—haiku and free verse—of Yosa Buson (1716–1783), one of three preeminent haiku poets of Japan. This, of course, like the earlier translation of Musō, was a collaboration, for I know no Japanese. Over ten years ago, Takako Lento, a Japanese American woman whose education had made her fluent in both languages, and who is a professional translator, sent me a sheaf of literal versions of haiku by Buson. She and I had worked together before over a few poems by modern Japanese poets, but never on an extended collection of the work of one poet. She asked me, when she sent the Buson, whether I was interested in working to make the literal versions of the haiku seem like poems written in English. I was fascinated by the haiku, and did what I could, keeping as close as possible to the literal meanings. We went on doing a few at a time, sporadically, for years, and I grew increasingly fond of Buson himself as I got to know him little by little. And in the end we had drafts of all of Buson's poems that have survived. We finished a working draft of the collection in 2011.

Takako and I celebrated finishing the collection, over a lunch at the Asia Society in New York, and I felt once again that I might have come to where I leave (for the time being) my practice of the impossible, unfinishable art, with gratitude for all that it may have taught me over the years, whether I knew it at the time or not.

Peahi, Maui, December 2011

Anonymous | Hawaiian
from the Hawaiian creation
chant *Kumulipo*

AT FIRST

From the turning the earth warmed
from the age turning the sky rolled
from the age in shadows the sun
to illumine the luminous moon
from the age of the Pleiades the night
from the age of the Small Eyes the night
from the slime welling up earth was becoming
from the welling of the dark the dark was
from the welling of the night the night was
from the dark was dark from the dark dark
from the dark of day from the dark of night
night only only

gave birth the night
gave birth to Kumulipo in the night a male
gave birth to Dark Welling in the night
dark Root Dark Welling in the night
dark Root Dark Spring in the night a male
gave birth to Po'ele in the night
to Night Dark in the night
Night Embryo Night Pool in the night a female

After the Martha Warren Beckwith
translation

Hadrian | Latin
A.D. 76–138

LITTLE SOUL

Little soul little stray
little drifter
now where will you stay
all pale and all alone
after the way
you used to make fun of things

2004

———————

Animula: A Late Visitation

It must have been at some time during my years at the university that I first encountered this brief, mysterious poem. It is ascribed to the Emperor Hadrian (A.D. 76–138) without any scholarly question that I know of, but it has always seemed surprising to me that a poem so assured in its art, so flawless and so haunting, could have been the only one he ever wrote. Perhaps he wrote poems all his life and this was the only one that was saved, or this one alone was unforgettable.

Certainly, whenever I read it first, I never forgot it, and I examined each of the translations of it into English as I came across them. The one I liked best was by Dudley Fitts. But it was the original poem that I was happy to return to, as any reader would who could do so.

Ten years or so after I left college I read Marguerite Yourcenar's novel *Memoirs of Hadrian*, in which the poem acquires a resonant imaginary context, memorable in itself, yet it was the original poem that I went on remembering, still ignorant of the circumstances in which it had come to exist. I am not certain whose soul the poem addresses, and as far as I know no one else can be sure of that either, though of course there are rooted assumptions about it.

Although I have tried to translate poetry (in full awareness of the limitations, the utter impossibility of the enterprise) ever since those student days, it never occurred to me to attempt to import this small solitaire. But in the past years poems have come to me arising from events that recalled the familiar Latin phrases, and one day I realized that I knew, suddenly, how I would like to hear the Latin phrases in English—if they could exist in English—and the words of the translation, as they occurred to me, seemed to be as literal as they could possibly be.

Horace

Latin
65–8 B.C.

1.20 (I.XX)

Your wine will be the ordinary Sabine
out of plain cups but I sealed it myself
in Greek wine jars and stored it on the day
    the theater thundered

for you, dear noble Maecenas, and thus the banks
of your native river and the Vatican
hill returned the happy repetition
    upon your recovery.

You can drink Caecuban and Calenian
vintages when you please, but my cups do not
know the taste of Falernian vineyards
    or Formian hillsides.

                         2002

1.31 (I.XXXI)

What does a poet ask at the new temple
to Apollo, and pray to have when pouring
    new wine from the bowl? Not for the piled
        harvests of opulent Sardinia

nor the contented herds in the warm climate
of Calabria, nor Indian gold or
    ivory, nor fields that the Liris
        wears away softly with its wordless flow.

Let those for whom Fortune provided it use
the pruning knife of Cales so that the rich
   merchant may drink from a golden bowl
      wine paid for with trade goods from Syria.

The gods seem to love that man. Three or four times
a year he sails out onto the Atlantic
   and survives. My own fare of olives,
      endives, and light mallow root suits me best.

Son of Latona, let me take pleasure in
what I have, keeping the health of my body
   and mind through a dignified old age,
      not lacking honor, or songs, to the end.

2002

Guilhem IX, Duke of Aquitane Occitan
1071-1126

With the sweetness of the new season
woods fill with leaves and the birds sing
each of them in its own tongue (*en lor lati*)
set to the verse of a new song,
then is the time a man should bring
himself to where his heart has gone.

From my best and fairest to me
no messenger nor seal I see
so my heart neither laughs nor sleeps
nor do I dare take further steps
until I know that we agree
it is as I want it to be.

The way this love of ours goes on
is like the branch of the hawthorn
that keeps trembling upon the tree
in the night in the rain and ice
until the sun comes and the day
spreads through the green leaves and branches.

I can still recall one morning
when we put an end to warring
and how great was the gift she then
gave me: her love and her ring.
God, just let me live to getting
my hand under her cloak again!

What do I care for the strange way
they talk to keep my love away?
I know how words are, how they go

everywhere, one hint is enough.
They talk of love, what do they know?
We have the morsel and the knife.

2001

I'll make a song of pure nothing,
not about me or another being,
not about love or being young
or anything.
It came to me while I was sleeping
on my horse riding.

The hour I was born is unknown to me.
I am not happy nor unhappy,
neither aloof nor friendly,
and the choice is not mine:
I am what a fairy made me
at night on a mountain.

I cannot say whether I
am asleep or awake. Somebody tell me.
My heart is nearly broken by
a pain I feel
for which I will not even sigh,
by Saint Martial.

I'm sick and fear that I will die
and all I know of it is hearsay.
I want a doctor who pleases me
I don't know who.
He'll be good if he can cure me;
if it gets worse, no.

I have a lover I don't know.
Never saw her. No use to.
No good or ill to me did she do
that I could notice
nor ever was Norman or Frenchman who
was in my house.

I never saw her but love her warmly.
I was never right and she never wronged me.
When I don't see her I manage nicely,
don't give a rooster.
I know one with more charm and beauty,
and her better.

I've made the verse, whose is unknown,
and I'll give it to that one
who'll pass it on to someone
going toward Anjou
so she'll send back a countersign
in his portmanteau.

2001

Now if I have the urge to sing
my sorrow will be what I sing
I will not bow to any king
in Limousin or Peitau again.

Now I must set out into exile
with great fear into great peril
leaving my son in war, and all
his neighbors set to do him evil.

It is anguish to go away
from Poitiers leaving the domain
and the welfare of his cousin
in the hands of Foulquet of Anjou.

If neither Foulquet of Anjou
nor my sovereign will help my son
I can guess what he will suffer
from Gascon thieves and Angevin.

If they think he is weak and young
when I am not here any more
they will have him down before long
unless he proves cunning and strong.

And I beg my companion's pardon
for every wrong that I have done her
as to Jesus on His throne
I pray my tongue and in Latin.

I was a man of strength and joy
but now we must part company
and I must make my way to Him
in whom all sinners end their sin.

I loved high spirits and loved laughing
our Lord wants no more of such things
I can take none of them along
as I come to the end of things.

To all I loved I say goodbye
goodbye to knighthood and to pride
so let it be as it pleases God
and I beg Him to welcome me.

May all my friends, after I die,
come with full hearts and honor me,
for I have known pleasure and joy
far away and in my own country.

So I take leave of joy and pleasure
sable and gray and ermine fur.

2010

SONG

When the flow of the fountain
flashes out into the sun
when the first wild roses open
and the nightingale upon
the bough rehearses yet again
the loving strain of his refrain
it is time to rehearse my own

love in a land so far away
for you I burn with my whole body
no medicine I know can soothe me
except the one that knows its way
out of your tender love to me
hidden under the orchard tree
wound in your longed-for company

it is no wonder that I burn
far beyond help from anyone
she is the most lovely Christian
Jewish maiden or Saracen
God ever made in His creation
he has known manna from heaven
to whom her love has been given

this passion never wanes in me
for the one I love completely
I fear she will be stolen from me
when others look at her with envy
one joy I know can take away
the pain that burns in me most fiercely
let no one feel sorry for me

even before it is set down
I sent this poem to be sung
by Filhol to Hugo le Brun
in our common roman tongue
may it bring joy to all who listen
through Peitau Berry and Garonne
as far as Brittany in the end

2010

Bernart de Ventadorn | Occitan
ca. 1135–ca. 1195

QUAN VEI L'ALAUZETA MOVER

When I see how the lark beats
his wings in joy at the sun's ray
when he forgets himself and lets
himself fall with sweetness of heart
oh I feel such envy for
anyone I see in joy
it is a wonder that my heart
does not melt with its desire.

Alas, I knew so much, I thought,
about love, and I knew so little!
For there is no way for me not
to love her who yields none at all.
She took herself and took my heart,
my self and all the world with her,
went and left only desire
and the longing of my heart.

The ladies bring me to despair,
I will not trust them any more.
Long I argued in their favor
but I will not any longer
for none is any use to me
with her who wastes and ruins me.
I have lost faith in all of them
knowing that they are all the same.

Love is lost, that much is certain,
and I never even knew it.
The one in whom it should have been
has none. Where can I look for it?

Oh it looks harsh to those who see her
let this poor creature pine for her
who finds no good except in her,
and die, since no help comes from her.

Since God is no help with my lady
nor mercy, nor what she should give me,
and since it is not her pleasure
to love me, I will never tell her,
and if she rejects and shuns me,
she kills me, and from death I answer.
I will leave, unless she keeps me,
exiled, despairing, who knows where.

I have no will of my own,
nor have been my own since she
let me look into her eyes,
into that mirror that enchants me.
Since in you, mirror, I have seen
myself I perish with deep sighs.
I lost myself there the same way
as fair Narcissus in the fountain.

In this my lady seems like all
the rest, and I blame her for that.
She does not want what she ought to,
and she does what she should not do.
I have crossed the bridge like a fool
and fallen into her ill will.
How it happened I cannot say
unless perhaps I climbed too high.

Tristan, you'll hear no more from me,
I leave and cannot say for where,
sad at heart, and will sing no more
but hide myself from love and joy.

2001

Anonymous trobairitz* | Occitan
late 12th or early 13th century

DIEUS SAL LA TERRA E.L PAIS

God save the land and country
where you have gone and now you are.
Be where I may, my heart is there
and no man over it has sway.
Oh that my body too were there
whatever anyone might say.
I would rather have perfect joy
than have him who desires me here.

---

*woman troubadour

Richard Coeur de Lion | French (Old French)
1157–1199

JA NUS HONS PRIS NE DIRA SA RESON

No prisoner ever said what he was thinking
straight out like someone who suffers nothing
but to ease his mind he can make a song.
My friends are many but are poor at giving.
It is their shame that, with no ransom coming,
these two winters I am held.

They know it well, my barons and my men,
English, Norman, Gascon, and Poitevin:
I never had so poor a companion
that I left him, to save money, in prison.
I say it not to reproach anyone,
but I am still held.

Now I can tell why dead men, as they say,
and prisoners, have no friends or family
since for silver and gold they abandon me.
It hurts me, but hurts my kin still more deeply,
for at my death they will be blamed severely
that I am so long held.

No wonder my heart is sore within me
when my own kin ravages my country.
If he had in mind the promise that we
swore, both of us, to keep mutually
I am certain that I would not long be
here confined and held.

They know full well in Anjou and Touraine,
who at this moment are rich, hale young men,
that I am far, and by strange hands held down.
They love me, but not with one gold grain.
Their splendid arms are missing on the plain
when I have long been held.

Some I have loved and love, comrades of mine,
from Caen some, and some from Percherain,
they tell me, song, cannot be counted on
though my heart toward them never was false or vain.
If they attack me now what a base thing will be done
when I am held.

Countess, sister, may your own sovereign virtue
save you and keep the one this plea is sent to
and by whom I am held.

I say none of this to the heir of Chartrain, who
is Louis's mother.

1948-2008

Dante Alighieri | Italian 1265-1321

CANZONE I

To the short day and the wide ring of shadow
    I have come alas and to the whitening of the hills
    when all the color has gone from the grass
    and yet my longing does not lose its green
    caught as it is in the hard stone
    that speaks and hears as though it were a woman

In the same fashion this strange woman
    stands frozen like snow in a shadow
    no more moved than if she were a stone
    by the sweet season that warms the hills
    and brings them again from white to green
    covering them with flowers and grass

When she wears on her head a garland of grass
    she banishes thought of every other woman
    for the waving gold mingling with the green
    is so lovely that Love lingers in her shadow
    she who has trapped me between little hills
    more tightly than if I were cast in stone

Her beauty has more power than any stone
    and what she strikes cannot be healed with grass
    so I have fled her over plains and hills
    trying to escape from such a woman
    and from her radiance nothing lent me shadow
    not hills nor walls and not the leaves' green

There was one time I saw her gowned in green
    so that she would have summoned from a stone
    that love that I have ever for her shadow

I loved her in a lovely field of grass
and she was as loving as ever any woman
and all around us was a ring of high hills

But the rivers surely will flow back to the hills
before this bough that is so soft and green
catches fire as a beautiful woman
from me who would be glad to sleep in stone
for the rest of my life and eat only grass
if I could watch where her skirt casts its shadow

When the hills cast their blackest shadow
under beautiful green this young woman
keeps it from sight like a stone hidden in grass

Versions over several years

FROM *LA VITA NUOVA*

O pilgrims who walk thinking it may be
of something that is not there now before you
do you come from people as far away
as it seems from the appearance of you
for you do not weep as you travel through
the center of a sorrowing city
as though you had come from a people who
have no awareness of her gravity

If you will stay hoping to learn of that
my mournful heart assures me beyond doubt
you will be weeping when you go away
She has lost her Beatrice and what
the words of anyone can say of that
can bring forth tears from those who hear of it

1990

FROM CANTO XXVI, *INFERNO*

"One shore and the other I saw as far as Spain,
far as Morocco, the isle of Sardinia
and the other islands that sea washes round.

I and my companions were old and near
the end when we came to the narrows
where Hercules set up his warning markers

for men, to tell them they should sail no farther.
On the right hand I left Seville behind,
on the other I had already left Ceuta.

'Oh brothers,' I said, 'who through a hundred
thousand perils have arrived at the west,
do not deny to the little waking

time that remains to your senses knowing
for yourselves the world on the far side
of the sun, that has no people in it.

Consider what you rose from: you were not
made to live like animals but
for the pursuit of virtue and knowledge.'

With this short speech I so whetted my
companions for the journey that I
would hardly have been able to hold them back,

and turning the stern toward the morning we
made wings of our oars for the insane flight,
bearing over the whole time toward the left.

Already the night could see all of the stars
of the other pole, and ours was so low
it never rose above the ocean floor.

Five times the light under the moon had been
lighted and as many times put out
since we had entered on the deep passage

when a mountain appeared dark in the distance
and it seemed to me that it was higher
than any I had ever seen before.

At the sight we rejoiced, but that turned quickly
to grief, for out of the new land a whirlwind
rose that struck the bow of our vessel.

Three times it spun her round with all the waters.
On the fourth it lifted the stern up
and drove down the prow, as pleased another,

until the sea was closed over us."

FROM CANTO XXVI, *PURGATORIO*

When my sight had feasted enough upon him
I offered my whole self at once to his service
with that earnestness that makes others believe.

And he to me, "You leave a mark so deep,
through what I hear, and see clearly, in me
that Lethe cannot wash it out nor fade it.

But if it is the truth that you have promised,
tell why it is that your face and speech
make it apparent that you hold me dear."

And I to him, "The sweet songs of yours
that so long as our present words endure
will make precious the ink in which they were written."

"Oh brother," he said, "the one at whom I am pointing
with my finger," indicating a spirit before him,
"was a better workman in the mother tongue:

verses of love and stories of romance,
he was peerless in all of them, and let the fools babble
who believe that the Limousin writes better.

They attend fashion rather than the truth,
and in that way they make up their opinion
before they give heed to art or reason.

That was the way many did with Guittone,
shout after shout all giving the prize to him
until the truth overcame most of them.

Now if so vast a privilege is yours
that you are free to walk on to the cloister
in which Christ is the abbot of the college,

recite to Him there a Paternoster for me,
insofar as we need one in this world
where the power to sin is ours no longer."

Then, it may be to make room for another
who was close to him, he vanished through the fire
like a fish going into the deepest water.

I moved forward a little toward the one
who had been pointed out and said to him
that my wish had made a welcome for his name.

Freely he began to speak to me:
"Your courteous question gives such pleasure to me
that I will not and cannot conceal myself from you.*

———

*In the original, Arnaut's speech is in Occitan.

I am Arnaut who weep and go singing.
With anguish of mind I see my old folly
and with joy see before me the hoped-for day.

Now I beg of you by that power
that is leading you to the top of the stair,
while there is time remember how I suffer!"

Then hid himself in the fire that refines them.

CANTO XXXIII, *PARADISO*

"Virgin mother, daughter of your son,
more lowly and more exalted than any creature,
the eternal counsel's fixed conclusion,

you are the one who so ennobled
human nature that the maker of it
condescended to be made of it.

In your womb the love was lit again
from whose warmth, in the eternal peace
this flower has been brought, thus, to open.

You are for us here the noonday torch
of charity, and there below, among
mortals, you are hope, its living spring.

You, lady, are so great and so availing
that whoever wants grace without turning
to you for it hopes to fly without a wing.

Your benevolence not only helps the one
who asks, but often it will run
freely to be ahead of the petition.

In you is mercy, in you is pity,
in you is bounty, in you, brought together,
all the good there is in any creature.

Now this one who, from the lowest hole
of the universe to here, has seen
the lives of the spirits one by one,

begs you, of your grace, for the power that will
allow him to lift his eyes up even
higher, turning toward the last salvation.

And I, who never burned for my own vision
more than I do for his, raise toward you all
my prayers, and pray they may not be too little,

for you, with your own prayers, to set him free
from every cloud of his mortality
and so disclose the supreme joy to him.

To you who can do all that you will, queen,
I pray, furthermore, that you will keep sound
his affections after all he has seen.

May your guard overcome human urges;
behold, with Beatrice, how many saints
for my prayers join toward you their hands."

The eyes that God delights in and reveres,
fixed upon the one who had made the prayer,
showed how dear devout prayers are to her.

Then they turned toward the eternal light
into which we must not believe the eye
of any creature can pass as clearly.

And I, who was coming close to the end
of all desires, within myself refined
appropriately the fire of my longing.

Bernard, with a smile, made me a sign
to look upward, but I was already,
of myself, as he wanted me to be,

for my vision entered, as it grew
pure, deeper and deeper into the beam
of the high light which of itself is true.

After that, what I saw was greater than
speech can portray, for at such a vision
it fails, and at that extreme, memory fails.

As one who sees when he is dreaming, and
after the dream the imprint of the passion
stays, and the rest does not come back to mind,

so am I, for almost all of my
vision has vanished, and still the sweetness born
from it is distilled in my heart to me.

Thus in the sun the snow loses its seal;
thus in the wind whatever oracle
the sibyl left on the light leaves is lost.

O highest light, lifted so far above
mortal conception, lend my mind again
a little of the way you appeared then

and to my tongue grant the ability
to leave to the people of the future
only one single spark of your glory,

for by returning to my memory
somewhat, and sounding in these lines a little,
more will be understood of your victory.

I believe that so piercing was the ray
which I endured that I would have been lost
if from it I had turned my eyes away.

And I remember that for that reason
I sustained it more boldly, until my vision
and the infinite goodness became one.

O grace abounding, that brought me to dare
direct my gaze through the eternal light
until I poured into it all my sight!

In its depths I saw that it contained,
by love into a single volume bound,
the scattered pages of the universe;

substances, accidents, and their relations
in such a way seemed to be mingled that
what I say is a simple glimmer of it.

I believe I saw the universal
form of this knot because I can feel
my joy expanding as I tell of it.

One moment brings me more oblivion
than five and twenty centuries brought upon
Neptune's wonder at the Argo's shadow.

So my mind, wholly caught up, went on
gazing with a fixed and motionless attention,
by its own gaze constantly kept burning.

One becomes such, in that light, that it would be
impossible ever to turn away
willingly to see anything else,

for the good, which is the object of the will,
is all there in it and what within it
is perfect is defective outside it.

From here on my tongue will fall even shorter,
with regard to what I can remember,
than an infant's still bathing at the breast.

Not because more than one simple aspect
was in the living light into which I gazed,
which is the same always as it was,

but through my sight which, as it gazed, was growing
stronger, one single appearance was taking
shape before me while I myself was changing.

Inside the deep and clear subsistence
of the exalted light three circles of three
colors and one magnitude appeared to me;

and the one seemed reflected in the other
as a rainbow in a rainbow, and the third seemed
fire breathed equally from one and the other.

Oh, how short speech falls, and how feeble
for my conception which, after what I saw,
cannot even be described as "little."

O light eternal who in yourself alone
abide, and alone know yourself and, known
to yourself, love and smile on yourself!

That circling which, conceived thus, came to be
seen in you as reflected light, when my
eyes studied it for a time, seemed to me,

within itself and in its own color,
to be painted with our own likeness
so that my sight was held completely there.

As the geometer who concentrates
on measuring the circle and cannot
find the needed principle in his thought,

so was I, at what I had just seen:
I wished to see how the image fitted
in the circle and what place it occupied,

but my wings had not been made for there,
although there was one flash that struck my mind,
bringing to it what it was wishing for.

Here power failed the high fantasy,
but my desire and will were turned already,
like a wheel that is moved evenly,

by the love that moves the sun and the other stars.

late 1990s

Petrarch | Italian 1304-1374

SONNET CCLXIX

Broken is the high column and green laurel tree
that formed in shade over my brooding mind.
I have lost what I do not hope to find
in the north wind or south or any sea.

You took from me, Death, my double treasure,
that made me live in joy and step proudly.
Not earth nor empire can restore it to me,
nor eastern jewel, nor gold, for all its power.

But in accepting that this has to be
what can I do but live with my soul's sadness,
eyes in tears always and a downcast face?

Oh life of ours, apparently so lovely,
how quickly, in a morning, we can lose
what years of suffering have won for us.

1990s

Joachim du Bellay | French
1522–1560

SONNET

You who have come to Rome in search of Rome
and cannot find the Rome you came to see
these ancient halls and arches that you see
and these old walls are what are now called Rome

Behold the pride and the decay and see
where she who held the whole world in her hand
from conquering was conquered in the end
devoured by time that to no one shows mercy

Rome is the only monument of Rome
Rome that by Rome alone was overcome
only the Tiber flowing to the sea

remains of Rome how contradictory
the world in which what stands firm falls away —
and what remains keeps leaving as it came.

1990s

We'll go to the woods no more
the laurels are all cut down

the beautiful woman there
will gather every one

    Come join the dance come dance
    arms around whom you please

The beautiful woman there
will she lead us in the dance

and the laurels in the wood
will we let them wither

No we will go one by one
and we will gather them

If the cicada is sleeping
no harm must come to him

The song of nightingale
will be what wakens him

And the warbler too
with his sweet ringing voice

And Jane the shepherd girl
with the white basket she carries

to gather strawberries
and the wild rose flowers

Cicada my cicada
come it is time to sing

the laurels of the wood
have all grown up again

2005

On the steps of the palace
on the steps of the palace

is a girl so beautiful lo la
is a girl so beautiful

So many in love with her
so many in love with her

she can't tell which to choose lo la
she can't tell which to choose

There's a little shoemaker
there's a little shoemaker

who's the one she likes best of all lo la
who's the one she likes best of all

Putting a slipper on her foot
putting a shoe on her foot

he told her what he wished lo la
he told her what he wishes

Beauty if you so please
beauty if you so please

we would sleep together lo la
we would sleep together

In a big four-cornered bed
in a big four-cornered bed

covered with fragrant white flowers lo la
covered with fragrant white flowers

At the four corners of the bed
at the four corners of the bed

bouquets of periwinkles lo la
bouquets of periwinkles

In the middle of the bed
in the middle of the bed

deep deep is the river lo la
deep deep is the river

All the horses of the king
all the horses of the king

could drink at the same time there lo la
could drink at the same time there

And there we two would sleep
and there we two would sleep

until the end of the world lo la
until the end of the world

ca. 2005

Aneirin | Welsh
ca. 6th century

FROM THE *GODODDIN*

Steady as a grown man
and yet a youth
ablaze for the fighting
fast stallions the manes flying
his legs gripping them
the light shield riding
the lean horse's flank
blue glint of blades
garments with gold borders
there will never be
bitterness between us
but I will make a song
of you for your fame
the field ran with his blood
before ever he was married
the crows ate their fill
before he was buried
Owain dear friend
covered with crows
the place haunts me with horror
Marro's one son was killed there

Diadem on his forehead
he rode always in front
he was tongue-tied before a girl
he paid for his feasting
his shield is broken
he bore down with the battle cry
on those who ran from him

he fought on while blood flowed
those who faced him he cut like rushes
in great halls the Gododdin will tell
of the return to Madawg's tent
where a hundred rode out only one came home

Diadem on his forehead
a wild wolf's rage
a string of amber at his throat
around and around
he was worth fine amber
in return for the wine he turned their blades back
with the blood running on them
men came from Gwynedd and Gogledd
at the bidding of Ysgyrran's son
and shields were broken to pieces

High were their hearts who went as one to Catraeth
they had drunk fresh mead and it was poison to them
there were three hundred of them drawn up for battle
and after the shouting there was silence
though they went to be forgiven in churches
the truth was that the hand of death was on them

Those who went to Catraeth in the first light
by their own high hearts they were cut off early
they drank the sweet gold mead that ensnared them
for one complete year there had been singing
red their swords leave the blades unwashed
their white shields four-sided spears
before Mynydawg Mwynfawr's men

Those who went to Catraeth were already famous
for all of one year they drank out of gold
wine and mead in honor of their calling
three hundred sixty-three of them in collars of twisted gold
of all those who charged after the mead was gone

three alone fought their way out of the battle
Aeron's two dogs of war and the rock Cynon
and I bleeding my way back to make my song

They went to Catraeth when the drinking was done
I would be ashamed not to sing their story
they fought with red spears they were hounds of war
they stood their ground wielding the dark heavy shafts
living would hardly be bearable to me
if I had left one of Brennych's band with life in him
I lost a friend there but I stood by him
he fought to the end and I grieve at leaving him
there was no dowry that he would come back for
he came from Maen Gwyngwn
Y Cair's last son

They went to Catraeth raising the battle shout
fast horses dark armor and shields
spears raised above them with the points sharpened
chain mail glinting swords flashing
one led the way pushing into the fight
five fifties went down before the blades that followed him
it was Rhufawn Hir who offered gold on the altar
and rewarded well those who sang for him

They went to Catraeth as the day began
there was one bringing bitterness to the enemy
they would need a bier to bear them away
no swords wilder than those that were with him
and never question of asking for quarter
when Neirthiad was leading the Gododdin
he showed the daring of his heart

There was one who went to Catraeth at first light
and a wall of shields rose around him
they charge they make way they lay hands on spoils
the crash of shields echoes like thunder

a burning man a man of judgment a champion
he plunged his spears and he tore with them
his blades butchered in welling blood
his iron came down on heads in the struggle
confronting Erthgi armies would cower

There was one who rushed to the battle
before the cows were awake
you had the way of a lion
the mead was gone there was only courage
a proud leader who would give no ground
son of Boddw Adaf renowned Eithinyn

They charged as one they rushed to be fighting
they were drunk with pure mead their lives were short
Mynydawg's men who won fame as warriors
for their fill of mead they laid down their lives
Cardawg and Madawg and Pyll and Ieuan
Gwgan and Gwiawn and Gwyn and Cynfan
Peredur with steel in his fist Gwawdur and Aeddan
where the fight swirled they stood firm and smashed shields
and though death bore them down they dealt it again
not one of them returned to what he knew

When you were famous for the way you fought
for our grain fields in the highlands
we were looked up to because we were with you
heavy door fortress for holding out
and a hand always for those who called to him
he was the tower in which the army trusted
wherever he was they called it heaven

As Catlew said no man
had a horse to catch Marchlew
he set spears in the thick of the fight
from a huge horse charging

not one to stand for the packsaddles
he struck out with a savage sword
with a fist like a block he dug in the ash-wood shafts
from the back of his foaming stallion
a beloved prince a free hand pouring the wine for us
swinging the whetted blade on which the blood flew
it was like the scything in haying weather
the way Marchlew let blood

His fame came from the south with him
Isaac whose ways were like a tide coming in
bounteous and open
fine friend to drink with
where his weapon went
a story ended
in his rage there was pure rage alone
his blade echoed in the heads of mothers
there was honor for Gwydneu's son
a wall in the battle

The one thing dearest the saddest loss
all for feasting all for a land
already taken and wasted
all for the hair that falls from a head
in the fight there was an eagle that was Gwydyen
he fought with his spear for Gwyddug
in the hands of a farmer
Morien's spear took out of the way
three wild boars with death before them
and Myrddin of the songs was with us
whose gift held up our hearts
when the walls rang and the fight tightened
with Saxons Irish Picts
and Gwenabwy fab Gwen the quick-handed
carried off Bradwen's rigid red body

I have not the burdens of the high-born
I am not looking for vengeance
my legs stretched out
under the crawlers
in the house of earth
an iron chain
around my ankles
brought on by mead by drinking horn
by the raid on Catraeth
I am not laughing
I Aneirin am not I
let Taliesin tell it
whom the words obey
I sang to the Gododdin
before the day

1990

Anonymous | Middle English
14th century

PATIENCE

Patience is a virtue, though few are fond of it.
When heavy hearts are hurt by scorn or other harm
Long-suffering may comfort them and soothe the burning,
For she quells all evil and quenches malice,
For if one could endure pain, happiness would come afterward,
So it is better to bear the blow to begin with
Than to struggle against it, however hard it seems.
I heard, on a holy day at a high mass
How Matthew told of his master teaching his followers.
Eight kinds of happiness he promised them, all of them rewards
Differing according to what each of them deserved.
They are happy that have poverty in their hearts
For theirs is the kingdom of heaven to have forever.
They are happy also that behave with meekness
For they shall possess this world and have their way.
They are happy also that weep for their hurt
For they shall obtain comfort of many kinds.
They are happy also that hunger after the right
For they shall be fully satisfied with every bounty.
They are happy also that have pity in their hearts
For mercy will reward them in every way.
They are happy also that are pure of heart
For with their own eyes they will see their Savior on the throne.
They are happy also that keep peace
For with grace they will be called sons of the gracious God.
They are happy also that can control their hearts
For theirs is the kingdom of heaven as I said before.
These are all eight of the happinesses that were promised to us
If we would love these ladies, emulating their virtues:
Dame Poverty, Dame Pity, and the third, Dame Repentance,

Dame Meekness, Dame Mercy, and Lovely Purity,
And then Dame Peace, and Patience, that were put in after them.
You would be happy with one of them. All would be better.
But since I must pay my respects to Poverty
I shall present Patience and so display both.
For there in the text these two are yoked together.
They are made into one meaning, first and last,
And pursuit of their wisdom earns the same reward,
And in my opinion they are of one nature.
For where Poverty pleases to be she will not be driven out
But stays where she wants to, whatever her welcome,
And where Poverty is oppressive, painful though it prove,
She must be endured, whatever may be said.
So Poverty and Patience must be play-fellows.
Since both have been given to me at once, I must bear it,
And would rather welcome my lot and speak well of it
Than struggle against it in anger and make it worse.
If there is a fixed destiny due to befall me
What is the good of maligning or opposing it?
Or if my liege Lord wants to send me
To ride or to run, roaming on his errand,
What can complaints do but make him angry?
He did not make me to be great, as I might have wished,
And I had to endure troubles as my reward.
I should have bowed to his bidding as I was bound to.
Did not Jonah in Judea try to trick him once,
To stay safe, and it brought him misfortune?
If you will be patient for a little, and listen a while,
I will let you hear how it went, as holy writ tells it.

        I

It happened one time within the confines of Judea:
Jonah was summoned from there as a prophet to the Gentiles.
When God's command came to him it made him unhappy.
It rang in his ear with a rough clang.

"Rise quickly," He says, "and leave here at once.
Make your way to Ninevah without another word,
And everywhere in that city tell them what I have said
Which I will put in your heart in that place, at that time.
For truly those who are living there are so wicked,
And so great is their malice that I will wait no longer
To take vengeance upon their evil and villainy.
Now go there quickly and take this message from me."
When that voice had ended, his mind was in turmoil.
It rose in a rage of rebellion, and he thought,
"If I bow to his bidding and bear this message to them,
And take myself to Ninevah, my troubles will begin.
He tells me those wicked people are hardened villains.
If I take them these tidings they will lay hold of me,
Pen me in a prison, put me in stocks,
Tie me down for torture, gouge out my eyes.
This is a mad message for a man to preach
Among so many enemies and merciless fiends
Unless my gracious God wants me to come to such grief,
To have me killed because of some sin of mine.
At all costs," the prophet said, "I will stay away from there.
I will go to some other place where he will not see me.
I shall travel into Tarshish and stay there for a while
And maybe when he has lost sight of me he will let me alone."
Then Jonah rises at once and hurries down
Toward the port of Jaffa, muttering with annoyance
At these troubles, with his mind made up not to endure them
Even if the father who formed him did not care about him.
"Our sire sits," he says, "on a seat so high
In his shining glory, it would not matter to him
If I were seized in Ninevah and stripped to the skin
And cruelly torn apart on a cross by a crowd of cutthroats."
So he goes down to that port to look for a vessel,
Finds a fine ship all ready to sail,
Makes friends with the mariners, pays for his passage
For them to take him right away to Tarshish.

Then he steps on board and they put up the mast,
Hoist the square sail, make fast the stays,
Heave at the windlass, weigh her anchors,
Loop the bowline smartly on the bowsprit,
Haul on the halyards—the mainsail falls.
They stood over to larboard to catch the wind.
The sail bellies out with the good breeze behind her.
They steer this sweet ship swiftly out of the harbor.
There had never been a more joyful Jew than Jonah was then
At having escaped the power of God so easily.
He was sure that the one who had fashioned the whole world
Was not able to trouble anyone, out on that sea.
Look at the poor fool, with such woes before him!
Now he has got himself into much deeper danger,
Holding in his mind the ignorant hope
That God could not see him once he was out of Samaria.
Oh yes, the one who loved him could see far and wide, surely.
And often he had heard the words of that king
Noble David on his dais, who had spoken thus
In a psalm that he made part of the Psalter:
"Oh foolish people, see things once as they are,
And come to your senses, fools though you may be.
Do you think that he who made all ears does not hear?
He who formed every eye cannot be blind."
But he fears no misfortune, in his fixed folly,
For he was far out at sea, hull-down for Tarshish.
Yet he was so quickly overtaken, it was clear
That he had shot shamefully short of his target.
For the Lord of understanding, who knows everything,
Always watching and waiting, has prepared his own plans.
He called upon creatures he himself had made.
They woke to anger, for he called in anger:
"Eurus and Aquilon, who live in the East,
Blow, both of you, I bid you, upon the gray waters."
Not a moment passed then between his word and their action,
So quick were they both to do as he ordered.

At once the noise begins from the northeast
As both the winds blew upon the gray waters.
Wild storm clouds rose up, red on the undersides.
The sea moaned in woe, a wonder to hear.
The winds on the dark waters wrestled together
Making the maddened waves roll and rise up high
Before they broke into the abyss so that the frightened fish
Did not dare to stay anywhere as the waves crashed on the sea floor.
When the wind and the sea and the boat came together
It was a joyless vessel that Jonah was in
For it reeled around upon the roiling waves.
The fierce wind blew from behind it and snapped all its rigging
Then hurled tiller and rudder on top of it,
Breaking the rest of the ropes first and the mast after them.
The sail swung onto the sea and then the craft
Caught its fill of cold water, and the cry goes up
To cut away the cords and cast them overboard.
Many hands fell to for bailing and emptying,
Scooping out the foul water to save their lives,
For though the way of it may be woeful, still a man's life is sweet.
They set themselves to casting all the cargo overboard,
Their bags and their feather beds and their bright clothing,
Their chests and their coffers and their casks, every one,
And all to lighten that vessel and save it if they could.
But the sound of the winds went on, as loud as ever,
And ever more angry was the water, and wilder the waves.
Then though they wearied themselves it did no good,
But each one cried out to that god he had his hope in.
Some swore solemn vows to Vernagu,
Some to devout Diana and bold Neptune,
To Mahomet and to Mergot, to the Moon and the Sun.
Then the cleverest of them spoke up, close to despair:
"I think we have some liar, some miserable outlaw here
Who has made his god angry and got in here among us.
Look, for his sin we are all sinking, and will be lost because of him.
I say we should draw lots, every one of us,

And whoever loses, we throw him overboard.
And when the guilty one is gone, a man may hope
That the ruler of the storm may take pity on the rest."
They agreed to that, and huddled together to do it,
Driven out of their corners to take what came to them.
A helmsman leapt briskly under the hatches
To fetch any from down below to draw their lots
And there was not a man who was missing
Except Jonah the Jew, curled up and hiding.
He had huddled down, afraid of the loud seas,
In the bottom of the boat, lying along a board,
Stretched out in the bilge, away from the wrath of heaven
And had fallen fast asleep, and was lying there snoring.
The fellow kicked him with his foot to make him get up:
The devil Raquel with his chains drive him from his dreams!
Then by the clasps of his clothes he clamps onto him,
And picked him up by the chest to set him on the deck
And asked him roughly what reason he had
To sleep so soundly with such disaster around him.
They get their lots ready then and deal them all around
And indeed the losing one ended up with Jonah.
Then they shouted at him, asking at the tops of their voices,
"What the devil have you done, you hopeless fool?
Why did you come to sea, you guilty sinner,
With such crimes upon you that you will destroy us all?
Have you no one guiding you, man, no god to call upon,
So that you slide off to sleep when you are close to being killed?
What country have you come from, what do you want here?
Where in the world are you going and what are you going for?
Look now: your doom awaits you for wickedness.
Glorify your god now, before you go from here."
"I am a Hebrew," he said, "born of Israel.
I worship the one who I believe made everything,
The whole world and the heavens, the wind and the stars,
And every living thing in it, with a single word.
All this trouble has come about now because of me,

For I have vexed my God and have been found guilty,
So throw me overboard and have done with me
Or you will never find fortune, and that is the truth."
He confessed to them until they understood
That he had fled from the face of almighty God.
Then such fear fell on them and panic possessed them
That they fell to the oars as let the man alone.
They ran out the long oars as fast as they could
To row on both sides, since their sail was lost.
They heaved and hauled, hoping to save themselves,
But it was all in vain and they gained nothing by it.
In the churning of the gray water their oars were broken.
Then they had nothing in their hands that might help them.
Then they had no hope, and did not know what to do
But send Jonah to his fate without waiting.
First they pray to the prince whom prophets serve
To grant them the grace never to displease him
Though their hands might be mingled in blameless blood
And though the man they killed belonged to him.
Then they took him up at once by head and by toe
And flung him straight out into the terrible water.
No sooner was he thrown than the storm stopped.
With that, the sea settled as soon as it could.
Then, though their rigging was ruined, ravelled on the waves,
Strong channelled currents forced them forward for a while,
Flinging them roughly ahead before the great swells
Until a gentler one lifted them swiftly onto the shore.
There was praise offered up, when they stood on land,
To our merciful God, after the manner of Moses,
With sacrifice made, and solemn vows,
Calling him the only God with no other beside him.
Though they were filled with joy, Jonah was in dread.
Though he wanted to have no trouble his soul is in danger.
For what happened to that man as he touched the water
Would be hard to believe were it not in holy writ.

Now Jonah the Jew is condemned to drown.
Then men hurried to hurl him off that shattered ship.
A wide rolling whale, as fate would have it,
Flung up from the abyss, was floating by that boat
And was aware of that man as the water reached for him,
And rushed to swallow him, opening his maw.
The people still had hold of his feet and the fish held him,
Threw him into his throat without a tooth touching him,
Then swiftly he slips down to the sea bottom
Past many jagged cliffs and streaming ledges
With the man in his maw dazed with dread,
And small wonder it was if he felt afraid.
For had not the high king of heaven, with the might of his hand,
Protected this wretch in the monster's bowel
What law could there be that would allow a man
To keep any life at all in there for that long?
But he was saved by that Sire who sits so high,
Though he could hope for no good in the belly of that fish,
And driven, besides, through the deep, rolling in the dark.
Lord! Cold was his comfort and his care huge
As he thought over all that had happened to him:
From the boat into the wild waves to be snatched by a beast
And flung into its throat all in a moment,
Like a mote in through a minster door, so vast were his jaws!
He slides in past the gills through rheum and slime,
Reeling down a bowel as though it were a road,
On, heel over head, spinning around
Until he blundered into a cavern as big as a hall
And there he sets his feet down and gropes around him
And stands up in the beast's stomach with its stink of the devil.
There in fat and feces that tasted of hell
His bower was built, who had wanted to be safe.
And then he lurks and looks for the best place to go
In every nook of that gut but he finds nowhere

Any rest of help, only filth and mire
In each gut he got to, but always God is sweet,
And there at last he came to a stop, and called upon the Lord:
"Now prince, have pity upon your prophet!
Though I may be foul and fickle and false in my heart
Be done with your vengeance now through the power of your mercy.
Though I may be guilty of guile, and a disgrace as a prophet,
You are God and all goods belong to you only.
Have mercy upon your man now, and his misdeeds
And show that you are lord truly on land and in water."
With that he went to a corner and settled down into it
Where he was not defiled by filth splashing over him.
There he stayed and was safe, though still in the dark
As in the hold of the boat where he had been sleeping before.
So in the bowel of that beast he stays waiting
Three days and nights, thinking only of God,
His might and his mercy and his moderation.
Now he knows him in woe as he could not in happiness
And all this while the whale rolls through the deep wilderness
Through many rough regions, by the strength of his will,
For that mote in his maw drove him on, I am sure:
Small though it seemed to him, it made him sick at heart.
And as the man sailed on he could hear the loud noise
Of the great sea on his back and beating along his sides.
Then came the moment when the prophet prayed
In this manner, I believe, with a rush of words:

III

"Lord, to you I have called in great trouble.
Out of the hole of the bowels of hell you heard me.
I called and you knew my voice, unclear though it was.
You plunged me into the dark heart of the deep sea.
The great rush of your flood folded around me.
All the currents of your chasms and bottomless abysses
And your streams, so many rivers roiling together

Into one rushing cataract roll over me,
And yet I said as I settled on the sea floor,
'My grief is that I am cast out from your clear eyes,
And cut off from your sight. Yet still I hope
To stand again in your temple, in your service.'
I am wrapped in water as my punishment.
The abyss binds the body that I abide in.
The wild crash of the waters plays upon my head.
I have fallen all the way to the foot of the mountain.
I am held back by barriers on every side
To keep me from any country, and you control my life.
You will save me, Sire, setting aside judgment
By the might of your mercy in which all our trust should be
For when the first stroke of anguish buried itself in my soul
Then in good time I remembered my great Lord,
Praying to him to have pity, to heed his prophet
And allow my plea to enter his holy house.
I have listened to your men of learning many a long day
But now I am certain that those unwise people
Who give themselves over to vanity and vain things
Forsake his mercy for things that amount to nothing.
But I make a solemn vow that will hold true
That I will make a sacrifice when I am saved
And offer you a rich gift for rescuing me,
And obey you, whatever you bid me do; here is my word!"
Then our father gave a stern command to the fish
To spit him up at once in a dry bare place.
The whale turns at his bidding and finds a shore
And vomits up the man there, as our Lord had told him to.
Then he was washed ashore in his filthy clothes—
He may well have wanted to wash his mantle.
The shore he saw, where he had come to rest,
Was in the very region where he had refused to go.
Then a wind of God's word came to reproach the man:
"Are you the one who would never go to Ninevah?"
"Yes, Lord," the man said, "grant me your grace

To go at your will; nothing else will help me."
"Rise. Go there to preach, then. See, this is the place.
See: my teaching is locked inside you. Let it be heard here."
Then the man rose up that very moment
And made his way before night to Ninevah.
It was a great city, spreading in every direction,
A full three days' journey from side to side.
Jonah travelled across it one whole day
Before he said a word to anyone,
And then he called out so loudly that they could all hear him
Putting the whole burden of his theme in these words:
"Forty days are all that are left before the end
And then shall Ninevah be taken and brought to nothing.
It is true that this very city shall fall to the ground
And plunge upside down into the abyss
And be swallowed up swiftly in the dark earth
And every living thing here shall lose its sweet life."
This speech leapt from him where he stood and spread around him
To the people of that city, the young men who lived there.
Such fear and terror took hold of them
That all their cheer changed and they were chilled at heart.
The man did not stop, but spoke on as before:
"The true vengeance of God will leave this place empty."
Then the people were silent and mourned piteously,
And in dread of God they grieved in their hearts.
They took out hair shirts that scratched them raw
And bound them to their backs and their bare sides,
Dropped dust on their heads and begged under their breaths
For their penance to please him, as they mourned for their sins.
He kept calling out through that country until the king heard him
And rose up in haste and ran from his throne.
He tore the rich robe off his naked back
And sat down in the middle of a heap of ashes.
He shouted for a hair shirt and tied it around himself,
Sewed a sackcloth over it, and groaned in grief.
There, dazed in that dust, with dropping tears,

He wept bitterly for the wrongs he had done.
Then he said to his servants, "Now gather around.
Issue a decree as I dictate it.
For every person living within this city,
Both men and beasts, women and children,
Each prince and priest and all the prelates,
To fast fervently for their false works.
Children are not to suck, however they cry.
No beasts are to graze on the broom or on the grassy plain.
They are not to be put out to pasture nor given gathered grasses.
No hay for the oxen, no horse to the water.
All shall cry out in salvation, with their whole strength.
The sound shall rise to him who will take pity.
Who can say what will be pleasing to the Lord
There in the heights where he governs us in grace?
Such is his might, I know, that though he may be displeased
Yet in his mildness he may find mercy.
And if we give up the habit of our loathsome sins
And keep to the way he himself set out for us,
He will turn from his anger and be done with his wrath
And forgive us this guilt, if we trust him as God."
Then they all believed in his law and left their sins,
Performed every penance the prince commanded,
And God in his goodness forgave, as he had promised.
Though he had pronounced sentence he withheld his judgment.

IV

Much sorrow settled then upon that man Jonah.
He was as wrathful as the wind toward our Lord.
With anger lashing in his heart he calls
In passion a prayer to the high prince, with these words:
"Now Sire, I beg you, judge for yourself:
Have not my own words been borne out now,
That I said in my own country when you commanded me
To come to this town to preach your message.
Well I knew your loving-kindness, your wise forbearance,

The bounty of your benevolence, and your good grace,
Your long-suffering with loss, your slowness to take vengeance,
And the fullness of your mercy always, however huge the offense.
I was sure that when I had said whatever I could
To warn all the proud people living in this city
For a prayer and penance they would be pardoned
And so I wanted to flee far off into Tarshish.
Now Lord, take away my life. It has lasted too long.
Bring me now to my deathbed and put an end to me,
For I think it would be sweeter to die at once
Than to preach your word any longer, since it makes me a liar."
The sound of our sovereign stirred in his ear then,
Upbraiding this man with fierce severity:
"Hear me, man! Have you any right to be so angry
At anything I ever did or said to you?"
Jonah gets up, all joyless and muttering,
And goes out to the east of the high town
And looks around the fields for a good place to settle
To wait and see what might happen next.
There he built himself a bower, as best he could,
Of hay and the common ferns and a few plants,
For that place was bare of swaying greenery
To shield against the glare or cast any shade.
He lay down in his little hut with his back to the sun
And there he slumbered and slept soundly the whole night.
While God, in his grace, grew from that soil
The loveliest vine over him that any man ever saw.
When the Almighty brought the day to dawning
Then the man woke up under the woodbine,
Looked up at the green foliage fluttering there.
No man ever had so sumptuous a bower,
For it was broad at the base, vaulted above,
Covered over on both sides like a house,
An opening on the north and no other anywhere
But all lapped in leaves whose shade kept it cool.
The man gazed at the green delicate leaves

Waving all the while in a cool, gentle wind.
The bright sun glittered through them, but not a single beam
Could shine, by so much as a mote, upon that man.
Then he was glad to have his lovely lodging,
To lie in lazily, looking toward the town,
So happy with his woodbine that he lolls around under it
All day without giving a devil's thought to his food.
And he kept laughing as he looked around his lodging
And wished it were in his own country so that he could live in it,
Up on Ephraim's or Hermon's hills.
"Indeed, a finer house I never found."
And when the night came on, and time for sleep,
He fell into a deep slumber under the leaves
While God fetched a worm that tunnelled the root
And by the time the man woke the woodbine was withered.
And then softly he wakens the west wind
And bids Zephyrus blow a warm breath
So that no cloud could come before the bright sun
So that it shone far and wide, burning like a candle.
Then the man woke out of his wandering dreams
And saw how his woodbine had come to ruin,
Its lovely leaves all faded and withered.
The bright sun had parched them before he was aware of it,
And then the heat had climbed and scorched them completely.
The hot wind from the west burns the roots.
The man groaned, on the ground, with nowhere to hide.
His woodbine was gone. He wept with grief.
In the heat of anger and rage he calls out,
"Oh maker of man, what good does it do you
To torment your servant worse than anyone, this way.
You never spare any harm you can do me.
I found one single comfort and now that is taken away:
My beautiful woodbine that covered my head.
But now I see that you want to rob me of every solace.
Why do you not give me my death? I have lived too long."
Yet the Lord spoke in answer to the man:
"Is this right, man, all this loud ranting,

Working up such a rage, suddenly, for a woodbine.
Why are you so sad, man, about so little?"
"It is not little," the man said. "It seems like a sentence.
I wish I were wrapped in the earth of this world."
"Then think, man, if you grieve so much for this,
Are you surprised that I help my own handiwork.
You are in such torment over your woodbine
Which you never spent a single hour caring for,
But which grew here one moment and was gone the next,
That in your anger you would throw your life away.
Then do not blame me for wanting to help what I have made
And for taking pity on those lost creatures who lament their sins.
First I formed them out of elements I myself had made
And then I watched over them a long time and led them on the way.
And if my labor should be lost after so long
And I were to destroy that town after they have repented
Sorrow would sink into my heart for so sweet a place
Where so many wicked men are repenting their evils,
Some of them no more sense in their heads
Than babies at the breast that never did harm,
And others foolish women who cannot tell
One hand from the other, for all this wide world,
Nor distinguish the rungs of a ladder from the side pieces,
Nor say what secret rule runs between the right hand
And the left though their lives depended on it.
And besides there are many dumb beasts in that town
That never sinned and have nothing to be sorry for.
Why should my anger fall on them, when some will yet turn
And come and know me for their king, and heed my words?
If I were as hasty as you in this, harm would come of it.
If my patience were no better than yours, few would prosper.
I cannot be so harsh and be called kind,
For sternness must be matched by mercy within."
Do not be so angry, good man, but go your ways.
Be restrained and patient in pain and joy.
For he that is too quick to tear his clothes
May come to sit in his rags sewing them back together.

So when poverty oppresses me, and pains torment me
I should endure it with long-suffering, patiently.
For repentance and pain finally prove
That patience is a noble virtue though few are fond of it.
    Amen.

2002

The Middle English original comes from one manuscript in the British Museum known as Cotton Nero A.x. (art. 3), named for the former owner, Sir R. Cotton, who had acquired it from the library of Henry Saville, of Yorkshire, "a great collector who secured spoils from northern monasteries and abbeys," in the time of Henry VIII and Elizabeth I. In the same manuscript, to which handwriting experts have ascribed a date close to 1400, are the sole surviving texts of three other poems (two of them, at least, among the greatest literary artifacts of the period): *Purity*, *Sir Gawain and the Green Knight*, and *Pearl*. Most scholars agree that all four of the poems were written by the same poet, whose name is unknown, and that the author came from the North Midlands, from Cheshire, Lancashire, or Yorkshire. If the same poet wrote them all, we do not know the order of their composition, but the transition from the alliterative early English line to the rhymed Romance stanza suggests that *Purity* and *Patience* came first, followed by *Sir Gawain* and *Pearl*.

While I was a college student, I found in a secondhand bookstore a copy of Henry Bateson's 1918 (second) edition of *Patience*, published by Manchester University Press. It had once belonged (in England, because penciled marks inside the front cover knock the price down from 2/6 to 1/) to someone named P.R.C. Potter, who had penciled English words above the originals, occasionally, in tiny script, already shadowy.

I blundered through the Middle English lines as well as I could, looking up word after word in the back—something that could hardly be called reading—and in this manner made my way through *Patience* before I approached *Sir Gawain* or *Pearl*. One image, a single phrase, from that first acquaintance with the poem, "Like a mote in through a minster door," never left me, and out of all of Middle English poetry continued to echo, and brought me back to the poem and to others of its time.

When I wanted to translate a few lines of *Patience*, I went back to the old Bateson edition that had been with me for years, and that is the edition I went on using. Bateson must have been working over his text during the years when J.R.R. Tolkien and E.V. Gordon were embarking on their studies of *Sir Gawain and the Green Knight*, referring to the same manuscript from more than five hundred years earlier. A mote in through a minster door.

The Green Knight takes his stand without lingering
And bends his head a little to show the skin.
He laid his long graceful locks across his crown,
Leaving the naked neck bare and ready.
Gawain gripped his ax and heaved it up high.
He set his left foot on the ground in front of him
And brought the blade down suddenly onto the bare skin
So that the sharp edge sundered the man's bones
And sank through the white flesh and sliced it in two
Until the bright steel of the bit sank into the ground.
The handsome head fell from the neck to the earth
And rolled out among their feet so that they kicked it.
The blood gushed from the body, glittering over the green,
And the knight never staggered or fell, for all that,
But he stepped forth as strong as ever, on unshaken legs,
And reached in roughly among the knights
To snatch up his lovely head and at once lift it high.
And then he turns to his horse and takes hold of the bridle,
Steps into the stirrup and swings himself up,
Holding his head in his hand by the hair,
And settles into the saddle as firmly as ever
With no trouble at all, though he sits there
       headless.
    All around him the blood sprayed
    As his gruesome body bled.
    Many of them were afraid
    When they heard what he said.

ca. 2000

"But have at it, knight, by your faith, and bring me to the point.
Deal me my destiny, and do it out of hand,
For I shall stand for your stroke and not flinch again
Until your ax strikes me, here is my word upon it."
"Have at you, then," the other said, and heaves it up high,
His face as fierce as that of a madman.
He aims a heavy blow at him but never touches him,
Withheld his hand suddenly before harm was done.
Gawain stood waiting for the blow, no part of him moving,
Still as a stone or as the stump of a tree
That a hundred roots have anchored in rocky ground.
Then merrily the man in green says to him,
"So now that you have your courage up I must make my stroke.
Uphold the high knighthood that Arthur bestowed on you
And see whether your neck can survive this blow."
Then Gawain was angry and in a rage he said,
"Well, strike then, you fierce fellow. Your threats take too long.
I begin to believe you are afraid of yourself."
"Indeed," that other knight said, "you speak so boldly,
I will not leave your mission unfulfilled
        any longer."
     Then he plants his feet to strike
     With set mouth and frowning brow.
     What was there for him to like
     With no hope of rescue?

ca. 2000

Dafydd ap Gwilym
Welsh
ca. 1320–ca. 1370

SINGING UNDER THE EAVES

The key is turned in the lock
listen to me love I'm sick
let me have a look
at you lovely for the sake
of God and His bounty
show yourself to me
what good will it do to lie
tell me in the name of Mary
don't make the kind of mistake
that could drive a man crazy

even one already crazy
with cold so that I struck
the door and at the third knock
the tight latch broke
every soul must have heard it
Morfudd my love with your mind set
on chastity as you put it
dangling it playing with it
no one so good at that
I have my bed made
just over the wall
you might try being merciful
with my fever I don't sleep at all
will you let a dark night
cheat us of joys that we might
come to and look at the state
I have come to standing out
in this weather coming down tonight

the eaves all one waterfall
running onto my skin
lashing his passion
and there is more snow than rain
now that is coming down
onto me and my desolation
I am past shivering
I think there is no mortal
style of suffering
worse than standing here awake
I swear by my maker
no bed was ever
this bad there was never
in the keep of Caernarfon
a worse dungeon
than I have here in the street

I don't want to spend the whole night here
for no one else would I do it
groaning suffering if I did not
love you I would not do it
in rain and snow night after night
not for a minute
for any but you would I do it
I would not have let
the whole world go
and with what pain I know
for anyone but you

here I am out
in the cold and you
have the luck to be in there
my pure soul is in there
that is my ghost out here
if anyone were to hear
of this it would be a wonder

to them my dear
that I am still alive here
my mind not stirring from here
crazy as ever to stay here

that promise to me from you
is what brought me where you are

ca. 2000

Eihei Dogen | Japanese
1200–1253

THE HOURS

Midnight: The Hour of the Rat (12 A.M.)

The barbarian knows
  he's not there yet
    but that's knowledge
Before midnight
  don't waste your thoughts
    on the transmission of the robe
Sit and cut off not only
  what appears within
    but the ultimate itself
Turn this over
  and make your bed
    and sleep

Cock Crow: The Hour of the Ox (1–3 A.M.)

The whole body
  is the self
    and the self is the whole body
How can you make
  the whole body bring back
    a single dream
Buddha belly
  and womb of ancestor
    pulse with life
Both shaggy-haired
  and horn-crowned
    can see far away and up close

Just Before Dawn: The Hour of the Tiger (3–5 A.M.)

Right at this
    moment
        don't be deceived
Six ears seven openings
    eight hollows—
        listen!
Now with no mouth
    the iron hammer
        exhales
But the whole of you
    realizes enlightenment
        with the morning star

Sunrise: The Hour of the Rabbit (5–7 A.M.)

Once you
    abandon your eyes
        you begin to see
Making nostrils
    for yourself
        how many do you need
Waiting for daylight
    in the snow-filled dark
        was it cold in the valley
The birth
    of the sun
        is the womb of the sun

Breakfast: The Hour of the Dragon (7–9 A.M.)

Eat the whole
    monks' hall
        swallow the Buddha hall
Soaring mind
    empty stomach
        at home in clouds and mist

Set the bowl down
        in India
                rinse it in Korea
Without asking
        Joshu
                all the rice and tea you want

Midmorning: The Hour of the Serpent (*9–11 A.M.*)

Nodding nodding
        going still farther
                the dragon reaches the water
Body and mind
        speak to each other
                for the grass it is spring
Greeting and answering
        there is no
                other face
Doing away with
        length and breadth
                no dust at all

Sun in the South: The Hour of the Horse (*11 A.M.–1 P.M.*)

At midpoint this
        sun is both
                bright and dark
Shining water
        the colors of spring
                light up the whole sky
I have been selling
        but I can buy
                just as well
At the market
        there's no stealing
                no mention of profit

Sun Reflected: The Hour of the Sheep (*1–3* P.M.)

> In the eye
>> of the sun's face
>>> the round face of the moon
> Coming to the sutra
>> covers the eye
>>> the eye becomes the sutra
> Study mastery
>> in the end
>>> there is nothing else
> Cloud in
>> the blue sky
>>> water in the jar

Midafternoon: The Hour of the Monkey (*3–5* P.M.)

> A foot
>> kicks over the oceans
>>> and the mountain peaks
> A clenched fist
>> summons
>>> the black clouds
> Suddenly thunder
>> rumbles and
>>> crashes
> Just sitting reflecting
>> attending
>>> the essence of mind

Sunset: The Hour of the Rooster (*5–7* P.M.)

> Look it's your
>> own son
>>> who's the thief
> Making up your mind
>> to strike the sky
>>> is the way of the hero

Are you determined
　　to master the direct
　　　　meaning
A gourd vine
　　all tangled up
　　　　in a gourd vine

Twilight: The Hour of the Dog (7–9 P.M.)

How can a dog
　　have no
　　　　dog nature
A frog's
　　whole body
　　　　is like a frog
A barefoot boy growing up
　　in China learns to walk
　　　　in Chinese
In India
　　King Prasenajit gives away
　　　　elephant tusks

Settling-In Time: The Hour of the Boar (9–11 P.M.)

Hitting the target
　　after the words have been spoken
　　　　is not good enough
Presenting the answer
　　before the occasion
　　　　is knowing spontaneously
Quick tongues
　　clear eyes
　　　　wide awake
Young lion
　　you snatched victory
　　　　from your adversary

1990, based on a literal
translation by Kazuaki Tanahashi

SNOW

All my life
        tangled in false and true
                right and wrong
admiring the moon
        laughing in the wind
                listening to birds
year after year wasted
        seeing a mountain
                covered with snow
only this winter
        I see the snow
                is the mountain

1980s, version adapted from
a literal translation by Kazuaki
Tanahashi and David Schneider

Yosa Buson | Japanese 1716–1783

In vain I listen
for the voice of the cuckoo
in the sky above the capital

> I had planned to go out
> but I stayed at home
> with the apricot flowers

I wonder who planted this
apricot tree with its white flowers
that's been outside the fence there since the old days

> Even with no light burning
> it looks as though someone's at home
> in the cottage among the apricot flowers

It doesn't go on from here
the narrow path ends
in the water parsley

LOOKING ACROSS THE FIELD

Mist in the grass
the water silent
just before sunset

> The spring rain is fanning on me
> I pull my old hood
> over old me

Spring rain
the day ending
I linger with it

Now that the geese have gone
the rice paddies in front of my door
seem far away

Grafting trees
they trade gossip
over the fence

Hoeing the field
in the hill's shadow
even the birds are still

Eating and sleeping
I wouldn't mind turning into a cow
the peach trees are in bloom

Sad not to find a note
after our night together
I hear the little cuckoo

A peony appears
in my mind
after the petals have fallen

This evening I cut
a peony stem
and felt my own spirit wither

The summer night is short
dew gathers
on the hairy caterpillars

AN OLD DOG

Okinamaro
are you still keeping watch
without sleep through the short summer nights

Washing my feet in a basin
I see that the basin leaks
water running out like the last of spring

A fish in an old well
leaps at mosquitoes
a sound of darkness

AT A PLACE CALLED KAYA IN TANGO REGION

This is happiness
crossing the stream in summer
carrying my straw sandals

The cut duckweed along the road
goes on flowering
in the evening rain

Ten wagonloads of sake barrel
sway along slowly
through the summer woods

All the way I have come
all the way I am going
here in this summer field

Mountain streams flow down
into each other
giving up their sounds

Fragrance of a sachet
the gesture of a young woman
who is mute

In the flash of lightning
I hear the dewdrops rolling
down the bamboo leaves

A wild boar lies down
on the valerian
dew gathers on the broken stems

The autumn chill becomes part of me
in the bedroom I step on a comb
that belonged to my dead wife

Under the harvest moon
a servant is on his way
to abandon a puppy

Memories of my father and mother
come to me all by themselves
late in the autumn

An autumn evening
sandpipers too
stand looking away

One step outside the gate
and I too am a traveller
on an evening in autumn

Some pilgrim drew eyes and nose
on a gourd
and went away

Beside the road
buckwheat flowers
flow over my hand

> How I love hearing
> the small birds
> up in the eaves

UPON MARYUNA'S REQUEST FOR A VERSE
TO GO ON HIS PAINTING OF A BLACK DOG

His bark comes
out of the darkness inside him
deep in the autumn night

> It is autumn in me
> but tomorrow will come
> and I will miss tonight

A bagworm hangs
snug and comfortable
in the first winter rain

> In silence the winter rain
> soaks the roots
> of the camphor tree

Is it a winter shower
or a mouse running
over the koto strings

> Old quick
> which shall I cover
> my head or my feet

BASHŌ'S TOMB AT KONPUKU-JI TEMPLE

I will die too
let me be a dry grass flower
here by the monument

      In the wild winter wind
      the voice of the water is torn
      falling across the rocks

I bury the charcoal embers
in the ashes
my hut is covered with snow

      I wear this hood
      rather than look as though
      I belonged to the drifting world

Silence
of an oak grove
the moon high in the trees

      A mouse peeps out
      eyeing the freezing oil
      of my lamp

Whenever I go to bed
with my socks on
I have bad dreams

PUTTING ON MY STRAW HAT AND
SANDALS FOR A JOURNEY

Since Bashō went
not a single year
has lived up to its promise

1990–2010, haiku translated with
Takako Lento

Jules Supervielle | French 1884-1960

FROM *OUBLIEUSE MÉMOIRE*

All at once my heart makes its way to the mountain.
Why are you going, and so far from me.
When you come back to me you are delirious
You edge sideways like a fugitive.

We will be without each other soon enough.
Then you will not be able to come back to me
But you will go knocking at every door
And no one will understand what you are saying.

Do not forget that only I understand
Your tangled speech which the words suffocate,
O you who have wanted to let me know
For some time now that you can do without me.

~

The world slips from me without a sound
Goodbye clever wood climbing from the root
And this dog that shakes its black fur and goes
And this bit of heat that escapes from me.

A ponderous procession leaves me night and day.
I am like a country deserted by the war,
Feeling cut off from the whole universe
Whose treasurer once it was, filled with love.

~

Do I need so many days to bring forth, one day,
What came to a point in me as in a book,
And for the dark being that flew in the black
Like a future bird to reach the plane of the light.

Yes I form the present from a flight to come,
Drawing it out of the listless past
And here is my always setting out from my pen
With all the sun and mist that it needs.

1990s

EURYDICE

Not to be able to turn
When the day is behind one,
When a night of deceit
Haunts our sentenced face,
When Eurydice's countenance
Making a dawn of delight
Shines on our back
But leaves our eyes without echoes,
Without a glimpse of the wonder
In full sail behind us.
One move is all it would take
For another world to come near,
For the darkness to answer
The questions of the heart.
But you cannot make a gesture.
A thousand iron hooks prevent you.
Nor even raise a hand
That would light up your way.

1990s

THE BATTLE CRY

The child copies out
colorless fractions
then in the glacial silence
of an occidental winter night
finally opens his history book
to Assas's battle cry
to an Auvergnat regiment
which he repeats for a moment
before he falls asleep.

THE GARDENS

Wearing oneself out looking for the secret of death
takes up time among the flower beds
of the gardens shimmering
with their red fruit
and their flowers.
One can feel this body of ours falling into ruin
without too much pain.
One bends to pick up
a coin no longer worth anything
overhearing in the distance
cries of pride or of love.
The fine sound of rakes
blends into the landscapes
traversed by the sighs
of those who are pulling
rampant weeds.

THE DAGGER

A traitor's old dagger
out of a melodrama
was found by a gloved hand
pulling up nettles.
The silence was vast and powerful
as in childhood
fields of apple trees
village flowers
narrow gates
composed a long evening
the color of the absolute
bathed the landscapes
pollen from a lily
had fallen onto the blade.

DOMESTIC LIFE

The woman washing herself
watched the yoked team
no grove's shade could have kept her skin fresh
the approach of death
and all of domestic life
seemed to be tied to the past of the world
vegetables scraped or peeled
to nourish beautiful girls
stone swept for a long time
in the fair summertime
animals bled in broad day
whose raw cry
melts away in the light.

WORDS

They were talking about
pretended love
at the old table
riddled with worms
the fire warmed up the stove
the lentil darkened as it cooked
and in the open doorway
facing human words
composed in well-tried syntax
the beauty of the bitter foliage
and birds with red breasts
were shining.

ABSENCE

The metal melts to marry the air
the consolation
forsakes a man
stroking the neck
of a draft horse
while gazing
at the cold plumage of the horizon.
One sees a single thread of smoke
one leaf taking wing
only the man has to know how long it will take.

RED ICE

In the year eighteen twelve in Russia
when the soldiers were retreating
among the corpses
of men and horses

the coarse wine had frozen
so the digger's ax
had to cut away
from the rest even from the dying
the block of red ice
in the shape of a barrel
which no museum
could have preserved.

THE RED APPLE

Tintoretto painted his dead daughter
in the distance carriages were passing
the painter died in his turn
nowadays long rails
lace in the earth
cutting into it
the Renaissance is still there
in the chiaroscuro of museums
the voices recede
sometimes even the silence
seems worn out
but the red apple is still there.

THE CRY

Parts of the fortified city
fall into neglect
a man stops
startled at the sound
of a voice breaking
in the insane asylum
the women there have to be bathed
one after the other
one who is still beautiful

prepares for it
though weeping without a sound
dogs worry
remains of a bone
in vain someone cries: Enough.

SHOELACE RETIED

When the evening launches
its mass of clouds
one sees the weed pile
send up its smoke
flowers grow in the gullies
there is a bit of day left
at that moment a boy
in iron-gray overalls
bends over the rut
to tie his shoelace
not weary of life
without a trace of absence.

THE DOOR

The day laborer bends to his hoe
until dark
he says a long time back
the cellar door
used to lock with
a pigtail bolt
now that's worn to death
he hears the way it screeches.
What future he asks
awaits us.
At his feet
the chained dogs sleep.

DOG DAY

In a country in Asia
they have a holiday once a year
for the dogs
put wreaths of flowers on them
red powder on their foreheads
the dogs sniff the air
look at the clouds as they did yesterday
each dressed up like the others
shivers and will die
knowing nothing about it.

SIGHTS

A patient stares
for a long time
at a drop of water
that holds the reflection
of a distant landscape.
A wine stain
the shape of France
stays on his face.
The foam on a glass
of bitter cider
subsides on a brown table
there is always
milk being boiled
just before dark
in this part of the world
where the eyes see
a moment far away.

1990s

Robert Melançon | French born 1947

THE LOVER [IV]

Night will exchange with day
its mass of darkness (magnificent
mane in which the stars shine) for
the details of the light. The Atlantic
will push back the Saint Lawrence, climbing its
current toward the five sweet-water seas
that are its inexhaustible source.
Evening will no longer deepen the streets
and autumn will flower more than May before
your face vanishes in me. But neither
the years nor the river nor the day
think of us whom they are carrying away.

BLIND PAINTER [XI]

January can give this grove
the appearance of a colonnade.
The fall of the leaves creates
a felicitous labyrinth, an architecture
to which only the light comes.
But you should not linger
in this metaphorical palace
old as language. Here are trees
all waiting to be named.
None looks like any other.
They will not consent to be reduced
to the mere concept of a forest.

NOVEMBER IN TOURAINE

Chameleon month, the motley wind
scatters you. You undress
by the Loire, you step down
into the water that reflects you,
you shake your tatters
voyager in one place. The season
will cover you with fogs in which you
will be lost, a season like the night rolling
at the rim of the horizon. The fields
the villages where you pass will be
given up to cold melancholy.
Your destitution will be where I stay.

AT DAWN

This hour when the night dissolves
before the day is formed
who has once seen it will not forget it.
It is the deep hour when the darkness
melts in the light that is not yet there.
You may have known before you were born
this uncertainty that tempts you
to hang back. But the day has to come
and with it death. Be happy. Gather it up.
Death and time will give you a face
then they will save you from it.

AUGUST

I wander beneath the serenity
of the moon as it withdraws
its stars from the night. A shadow
goes with me in which I do not
know myself. Only these trees
nearest to me, the grass, the washed darkness
exist. A cry
of a nightjar, the murmur of leaves.
Summer consents absently to the night.

THE LOVER [IX]

As long as the snow lights the winter
as long as the day alternates
with the night that pursues and flees it
as long as the streets fill with sounds
and as long as the Saint Lawrence flows between
its banks without waiting for anything
with Montreal passing upside down in
its mists I will be yours.
But we will pass like the snow
like the light and the darkness
with this city and its river
which will flow long after us
as though we had never been.

1990s

Gustavo Bécquer | Spanish 1836–1870

THE RETURNING SWALLOWS

They will come back the dark swallows
to hang their nests inside your balcony
and again around your mirrors they
    will flash their wings in play

but those that paused in flight to contemplate
your beauty and what I said to you
the ones that had our names by memory
    they will not come again

They will come back the clustering honeysuckles
to climb the clay walls around your garden
and again more lovely still toward the day's end
    their flowers will open

but the ones that were together in the dew
whose drops we were watching when they trembled
and fell as though they were the tears of day
    they will not come again

They will come again those ardent words
of love and they will echo in your ears
and it may be that from the depths of sleep
    your heart will waken

but speechless and spellbound and upon knees
as God is worshipped before his altar
as I have loved you—never imagine
    any will love you so

2005

Jorge Luis Borges | Spanish 1899–1986

EVENING

The evenings to come and those that have been
are all one, inconceivably.
They are a clear crystal, alone and suffering,
inaccessible to time and its forgetting.
They are the mirrors of that eternal evening
that is treasured in a secret heaven.
In that heaven are the fish, the dawn,
the scales, the sword, and the cistern.
Each one an archetype. So Plotinus
teaches us in his books, which are nine.
It may be that our brief life
is the fleeting reflection of the divine.
The elemental evening encircles the house.
Yesterday's, today's, the one that is always there.

2010

SOUTH

To have watched from one of your patios
the ancient stars
from the bank of shadow to have watched
the scattered lights
my ignorance has learned no names for
nor their places in constellations
to have heard the ring of water in the secret pool
known the scent of jasmine and honeysuckle
the silence of the sleeping bird
the arch of the entrance the damp
—these very things may be the poem.

1980s

THE LABYRINTH

Zeus would not be able to take away
the stone nets that surround me. I have forgotten
the man I used to be. I follow
the hated road of monotonous walls
that is my destiny. Stacked galleries
that circle in secret orbits at the ends
of the years. Parapets cracked
by the wear of the days. In the pallid
dust I have deciphered tracks that fill me
with dread. Through the concave afternoons
the air has carried to me a bellowing
a desolate bellowing or its echo.
I know that in the shadow there is an Other
whose lot it is to wait out the long solitudes
woven and unwoven by this Hades
and to thirst for my blood and devour my death.
We are looking for each other. Oh if only
this were the last day of waiting.

1980s

BLAKE

Where can it be, the rose
that in your hand, without knowing it
lavished intimate gifts?
It is not in the color, because the flower is
     blind,
nor in the sweet inexhaustible scent
nor in the weight of a petal. These things
are a few traceless echoes.
The true rose is far away.
It may be a column or a battle

or a firmament with angels in an infinite
world, secret and necessary,
or the rejoicing of a god, which we
      do not see,
or a silver planet in another sky,
or a terrible archetype,
not like a rose at all.

2011

Pablo Antonio Cuadra | Spanish 1912–2002

HUMMING ON THE WHARF

The young women
admire
  the setting sun.
They worry
about the clouds
ugly clouds
menacing the night.
The young women
     sing
pure voices
and I troll the hook
through the swollen
water.
      The young women
      who are in love
        wait for someone
        all afternoon.
The fish are not biting
and the day
goes down hungry.

THE PAIN

What tells me to start
fingering the harp strings?—
already in me
the pain of distance begins.
One

Sail

    a long way out

        is all it takes.

SONG FOR THOSE GIRLS

Thinking there is no one around
those girls dance naked on the glittering sand
in time with the waves.

What will I do next time I see them
when I come at night and they saying nothing
and I ponder their silence
sitting there in the firelight
and my dark stubborn heart jumps up like a dog
snatching at the memory of their bare bodies?

VOICES

At night
while we sailed
we were listening to songs
far away on the shore.

    A star wounded the spot
      where the three daughters
        of Tarca were shipwrecked.
          All of them played the guitar.

THE MASTER OF TARCA [1]

Sitting on the Eagle Stone, the master of Tarca said
to us

It is the way it was meant to be
        it is right
    for the sailor
    to grasp
things by their names.
    In time of danger
it is the things with no names
    that do the harm.

THE GIRLS

The girls from the archipelago
are rowing home after mass.
Like flowers floating
like garlands
of happy colors.
Say goodbye to them
from your island
and you will raise a flight
of voices clear
as birds.

THE COWBOY FROM APOMPOA

Telen
Rodrigues
cowboy
from Apompoa.
That night

he came to sing
to Rosa Reyes.

Didn't want
to drink. Remained
silent
and we slept.

When we reached
port nobody knew
what had become of him. He fell
into the water. That's
what they said.

Later I knew
Rosa
Reyes. She was
beautiful and crazy.

When Telen
sang his serenade
she was sleeping
with Victor
the one from Tisea.

All was secret
    and music
        was playing when
Victor's horse
    neighed
in the cornfield.

THE MASTER OF TARCA [III]

Master, Cifar said,
     I did what you told me to do
     and crossed the Lake
looking for the unknown island.
     A good wind took me
to the farthest one, virgin and lost.
       But
     I knew that island
       I would swear it.
     It was the same woman
who was waiting for me there
     I would almost swear it.
The master smiled and said
      The known
     is the unknown.

ABDUCTION

Above the peaks
in a pale sky
     the morning star is shining.

I let go the anchor and at the sound
the birds scream.
     Herons are flying
the sheep in the flocks are bleating
far away is a hollow in the sand.
Fidelia comes out on deck
combing her hair
in the cool of the morning.
     She came with me
      last night. They

fired at me, then came after me
    with fast boats. But
      The Siren can move.

I have an island for her.

THE CHILD

The child
that I was
never died
he is still there
    in my breast
      he takes the heart
for his own
and sails inside
I hear him crossing
    my nights
    or his old
    flood of tears
    sweeps me along
    through the dream.

THE EMPTY ISLAND

The trees
that held on to the moon
still cling
to it with
their shadow
and the same songs are born
of the wind
among the branches.
By the short path

from your house to the water
your clothes are
not spread now, but the flowers
have survived. Everything is the same.
Even so
I regret having dropped anchor
in the sandy
bay of your
island.

THE BLACK SHIP

In his dream Cifar heard the shouts
and the conch hooting in the fog
at dawn. He looked at the ship
       motionless
       not rocking among the waves.

    —If you hear
    in the dark core
    of the night
    when the sea is high
    shouts asking
    the way to the harbor
        come about hard
        and get out of there.

Silhouetted on the spray
hull dark and rotted away
(Sailor! they shouted)
the rigging in tatters
swinging and the sails
black and in rags
       (Sailor!)
Cifar stood up and clung to the mast.

—If the moon
shines on their faces
with the long beards
if they say to you
—Sailor, where are we headed.
If they beg you:
—Sailor, show me
the way to the harbor!
come about hard
and get out of there.

A long time they have been sailing.
Centuries they have been voyaging in the dream.

They are your own questions
lost in time.

1980s, preceding poems are from
Cantos de Cifar

THE CEIBA*

When our ancestors came

— *"and they came because in that country*
they had masters for whom they worked
and who mistreated them"—

they climbed the great tree on the day that its fruit opens
and they blew on its flying seeds to find out the way of exodus.
And some seeds took the way of the birds that feed on worms
and others the way of the small birds that fly as one and feed on seeds
and others took the way of the vultures and turkey buzzards that live
     on carrion

———
*This is the silk cotton tree (*Ceiba pentandra *or* Eriodendron anfractuosum*) aka the
God Tree.

and from their height, each alone, see death
and others took the way of the eagles and condors, the highest of all,
that is crossed only by the butterflies and the thoughts of the thinkers.

    This is the tree of contradiction.
This is the *Vahonché* that Landa mentioned and "which means a lofty
    trunk with the power to withstand demons."
This is the gigantic tree that Gómara saw and fifteen men clasping each
    other's hands could not embrace it.
    This is the tree of the Trévedes that Oviedo says was taller than
        the tower of San Román in the city of Toledo.
And it is the one that Núñez de la Vega says all the inhabitants of this
    land have in their marketplaces
and under them they hold their meetings
and they burn incense to them in braziers because it is their belief
that they are descended from the roots of the Ceiba.

    I have remembered its ancient shadow circling around this city
      in ruins.
In Candelaria Street where my house was
—I mean the old house where I was born—
now there is not one stone left upon another.
        And the moon
        that white crow
        saying Never again!

I have remembered its ancient shadow here where there is not
    enough love
to raise the stones.
      Come out of the stones, my people!
A new roof covers your exiles. A beam
extends its branches.
      This is
what was foretold in the book of the prophets of Chumayel:
"Yaax-Imixché, the Green Ceiba, will rise up in the center of
    the province.
as a sign and reminder of the annihilation."

Where this Tree is born is the center of the world.
What you see from its crown is what your heart longs for.
    This is the tree that sets your children tenderly on its knees.
With the light silky cotton of its fruit our people made their pillows
on which they could stretch out to rest and elaborate their dreams.
    If the serpent climbs this tree it turns into a bird and if a word climbs
this tree it turns into a song.
    This is the Mother Ceiba in whose swollen trunk your people
        revered
pregnancy and fertility. From a single piece of its white wood, easy to
    carve, they made a vessel to set out in, and that embarkation is
        their cradle
when they start their voyage and their coffin when they reach port.
    From this tree man learned mercy and architecture, liberality
        and order.

April 2003

Alberto Blanco | Spanish <br> born 1951

THE PARAKEETS

They talk all day
and when it starts to get dark
they lower their voices
to converse with their own shadows
and with the silence.

They are like everybody
        —the parakeets—
all day chatter,
and at night bad dreams.

With their gold rings
on their clever faces,
brilliant feathers
and the heart restless
with speech…

They are like everybody
        —the parakeets—
the ones that talk best
have separate cages.

1995

THE SWALLOW

The enormous relief we feel
as we look at the distant mountains,
watch the flight of a swallow,
listen to the voice
of the wind in the ash trees,
comes from touching for a moment
as a member of the same family
beings beyond number
that are nothing but what they are
and have no wish
to be anything else.

2000

W.S. Merwin's honors include the Bollingen Prize, two Pulitzer Prizes, the Aiken Taylor Award for Modern American Poetry, the Ruth Lilly Poetry Prize, the PEN Translation Prize, the Shelley Memorial Award, the Wallace Stevens Award, and a Lila Wallace-Reader's Digest Writers' Award. He has also been awarded fellowships from The Academy of American Poets, the Guggenheim Foundation, the National Endowment for the Arts, and the Rockefeller Foundation. Merwin is a former Chancellor of The Academy of American Poets and has served as Special Consultant in Poetry to the Library of Congress in 1999–2000 and as Poet Laureate in 2010–2011.

ACKNOWLEDGMENTS

"I'll Make a song of pure nothing," "No prisoner ever said what he was thinking," "Now when I feel the will to sing," "When I hear how the lark beats," and "With the Sweetness of the New Season" reprinted with the permission of the National Geographic Society from the book *The Mays of Ventadorn*, by W.S. Merwin. Copyright © 2002 W.S. Merwin.

"Blake" from *Poesía Completa* by Jorge Luis Borges. Copyright © 1995 by Maria Kodama, used by permission of the Wylie Agency LLC.

"I.xx" and "I.xxxi" from *Horace, the Odes: New Translations by Contemporary Poets*, copyright © Princeton University Press.

"The Afternoon," translated by W.S. Merwin, copyright © 1999 by Maria Kodama; translation copyright © 1999 by W.S. Merwin, "The South," translated by W.S. Merwin, copyright © 1999 by Maria Kodama; translation copyright © 1999 by W.S. Merwin, "The Labyrinth," translated by Stephen Kessler, copyright © 1999 by Maria Kodama; translation copyright © 1999 by Stephen Kessler, "My Whole Life," translated by W.S. Merwin, copyright © 1999 by Maria Kodama; translation copyright © 1999 by W.S. Merwin, "To a Minor Poet of the Greek Anthology," translated by W.S. Merwin, copyright © 1999 by Maria Kodama; translation copyright © by W.S. Merwin; "The Poet Proclaims His Renown," translated by Kenneth Krabbenhoft, copyright © by Maria Kodama; translation © 1999 by Kenneth Krabbenhoft, "Parting," translated by W.S. Merwin, copyright © 1999 by Maria Kodama; translation copyright © by W.S. Merwin, "The Generous Friend," translated by Kenneth Krabbenhoft, copyright © 1999 by Maria Kodama; translation copyright © 1999 by Kenneth Krabbenhoft, from *Selected Poems by Jorge Luis Borges*, edited by Alexander Coleman. Used by permission of Viking Penguin, a division of Penguin Group (USA) Inc.

Copper Canyon Press is grateful to the following individuals whose extraordinary support made the publication of *Selected Translations* by W.S. Merwin possible.

Joseph Bednarik

Amelia Bentley

John Branch

Valerie Brewster

David G. Brewster and
Mary Kay Sneeringer

Diana and Jay Broze

David Caligiuri

Lance Conn

Janet and Leslie Cox

Vasiliki Dwyer

Kelly Forsythe

Mimi Gardner Gates

Daniel Gerber

Kip Robinson Greenthal and
Stanley Greenthal

Margaret Kirk

George Knotek

Rhoady and Jeanne Marie Lee

Maureen Lee and Mark Busto

Jayne Lindley

Mary Lindley

Brice Marden

Ken Masters

Christopher Overman

H. Stewart Parker

Penny and Jerry Peabody

John Pierce

Victoria Poling

Joseph C. Roberts

Larry Rouch

Pamela Sampel

Daniel Schreiber

Cynthia Lovelace Sears and
Frank Buxton

Rick Simonson

Randy Sturgis

Tonaya Thompson

William and Ruth True

Daniel Waggoner

Austin Walters

Michael Wiegers

Poetry is vital to language and living. Since 1972, Copper Canyon Press has published extraordinary poetry from around the world to engage the imaginations and intellects of readers, writers, booksellers, librarians, teachers, students, and donors.

WE ARE GRATEFUL FOR THE MAJOR SUPPORT PROVIDED BY:

THE PAUL G. ALLEN
FAMILY FOUNDATION

THE MAURER FAMILY
FOUNDATION

NATIONAL
ENDOWMENT
FOR THE ARTS

WASHINGTON STATE
ARTS COMMISSION

Anonymous

Arcadia Fund

John Branch

Diana and Jay Broze

Beroz Ferrell & The Point, LLC

Mimi Gardner Gates

Gull Industries, Inc.
on behalf of William and Ruth True

Mark Hamilton and Suzie Rapp

Carolyn and Robert Hedin

Steven Myron Holl

Rhoady and Jeanne Marie Lee

Maureen Lee and Mark Busto

New Mexico Community Foundation

H. Stewart Parker

Penny and Jerry Peabody

Joseph C. Roberts

Cynthia Lovelace Sears and Frank Buxton

The Seattle Foundation

Charles and Barbara Wright

The dedicated interns and faithful
volunteers of Copper Canyon Press

To learn more about underwriting Copper Canyon Press titles,
please call 360-385-4925 ext. 103

The Chinese character for poetry is made up of two parts: "word" and "temple." It also serves as pressmark for Copper Canyon Press.

The typeface is Janson Text, created by Hungarian travelling scholar Nicholas Kis in the late 1680s while Kis worked in Anton Janson's Amsterdam workshop. Display type is Hoefler Titling, a contemporary reworking of Janson Text and other baroque type designs. Book design and composition by Valerie Brewster. Printed on archival-quality paper at McNaughton & Gunn, Inc.